RE

book
kee

How to ke
and cost-

Martin Quinn

Prentice Hall
is an imprint of

PEARSON

Harlow, England • London • New York • Boston • San Francisco • Toronto • Sydney • Singapore • Hong Kong
Tokyo • Seoul • Taipei • New Delhi • Cape Town • Madrid • Mexico City • Amsterdam • Munich • Paris • Milan

PEARSON EDUCATION LIMITED

Edinburgh Gate

Harlow CM20 2JE

Tel: +44 (0)1279 623623

Fax: +44 (0)1279 431059

Website: www.pearsoned.co.uk

First published in Great Britain in 2010

© Pearson Education Limited 2010

The right of Martin Quinn to be identified as author of this work has been asserted by him in accordance with the Copyright, Designs and Patents Act 1988.

ISBN: 978-0-273-73178-8

British Library Cataloguing-in-Publication Data

A catalogue record for this book is available from the British Library

Library of Congress Cataloging-in-Publication Data

Quinn, Martin, 1973–

  Brilliant book-keeping: what the best book-keepers know, do and say / Martin Quinn.

    p. cm.

  ISBN 978-0-273-73178-8 (pbk.)

 1. Bookkeeping. 2. Accounting. I. Title. II. Title: Brilliant bookkeeping.

  HF5636.Q853 2010

  657'.2--dc22

                                                                        2010008545

10 9 8 7 6 5 4 3 2 1

14 13 12 11 10

Typeset in 10/14pt Plantin by 3

Printed and bound in Great Britain by Henry Ling Ltd, Dorchester, Dorset

For my parents, William and Anne

Contents

About the author

Martin Quinn is a lecturer in accounting at Dublin City University. He is also a Chartered Management Accountant with 12 years' experience in both accounting practice and industry.

For the past five years, Martin has been teaching the accountants of the future. In his teaching, he has a firm belief in getting the basics right first. More complex topics will then be easier to appreciate. He also advises many small businesses on how to get their book-keeping right from the outset.

Martin is author of *Book-keeping and Accounts for Entrepreneurs*, also from Pearson and has contributed to a number of academic textbooks. His blog – martinjquinn.com – provides regular pieces on book-keeping and accounting issues.

Acknowledgements

I'd like to thank those who helped me to learn about accounting and book-keeping as a young trainee accountant – Dermot, Chris and Gary. Having learned it in theory, you guys showed me how it's really done.

Thanks to my wife and children, without whom life would be a lot less interesting.

And last, but by no means least, thanks to Caroline and all the other staff at Pearson, who have always been a great help in getting my books to print.

Publisher's acknowledgements

We are grateful to the following for permission to reproduce screenshots:

Figures 3.4, 3.5, 3.6, 3.7, 4.2, 4.3, 4.4, 4.6, 4.7, 4.8, 4.9, 5.3, 5.4, 5.5, 5.6, 5.8, 5.9, 5.10, 5.11, 7.2, 7.5, 7.6, 7.7, 7.8, 7.9, 7.10, 8.10, 8.11, 9.7, 9.8, 9.9. Screenshots © Intuit Inc. All rights reserved.

Figures 6.1, 6.2, 6.3, 6.4 reproduced by permission of 12Pay.

Introduction

If you run your own small business, you'll already know that book-keeping is crucial to a successful business. It's one of the most important things for any business to do well. Otherwise, it's impossible to assess costs, revenues and keep a handle on how much money is being made in a business.

Book-keeping is in fact a relatively simple task. There are a few key underlying principles in the book-keeping and accounting world and, once you know these, you're off to a great start. Yes, there are some concepts you'll need to understand, but you'll pick them up as you progress through this book.

So what is book-keeping? First a book-keeper is someone who records the accounts or transactions of a business. Book-keeping is then what a book-keeper does; in other words capturing the data from day-to-day business transactions such as sales, purchases, receipts and payments. Incidentally, the word 'book-keeper' dates back to the sixteenth century, so it is an old and well-practised profession.

As book-keeping captures and records the transactions of an organisation, it is a crucial part of understanding what is happening in that organisation, be it a business, charity, other form of organisation or your own personal finances. It is the key source of information for the owners of a business, helping them to find out how much money they made, how much money they are owed, how much money they owe, how much they sold, etc. This information is important for others too, such as potential investors, employees, banks and, of course, the tax authorities.

In *Brilliant book-keeping* you'll learn the concepts of book-keeping and how to keep good records in your own business or in your job as book-keeper. *Brilliant book-keeping* is divided into four parts. Part 1 (Chapters 1 and 2) introduces some basic concepts underlying book-keeping and accounting. You'll get more details on what book-keeping entails and then see some advantages of doing the book-keeping work yourself within a business, as opposed to engaging an accountant. Part 2 (Chapters 3 to 7) gets straight into the recording of business transactions. A separate chapter will explain how transactions relating to sales, purchases, receipts, payments, employees and assets are captured and recorded. This part will first show you how to record data manually, using hardback journals or spreadsheets. Once this knowledge is on board, you'll see some accounting software which can make book-keeping tasks a whole lot easier. Part 3 (Chapters 8 and 9) then describes what happens to the recorded data (from sales, purchases, etc.) or, in other words, how it is summarised and turned into useful information. How data recorded is transferred to ledgers is detailed, and how the ledgers are used to prepare two important accounting reports – the income statement (profit and loss account) and the balance sheet. Finally, Part 4 gives some tips on how to keep your records accurate and ensure that all reports produced are reflective of the underlying transactions. These tips will help you to be confident in what you do and to ensure that your accountant, bank manager or tax inspector will be happy.

Brilliant book-keeping is packed with useful, practical examples which will help you get to grips with key book-keeping concepts. Remember, practice makes perfect, so why not take the records of your business (or the business you work in) and start practising straight away. If you are completely new to book-keeping but existing records are in place, why not try to re-do the records yourself? So get cracking as soon as you can.

Finally, *Brilliant book-keeping* normally refers to book-keeping in businesses, or what are called 'for-profit' organisations. However, most of the material will also be relevant to 'not-for-profit' organisations such as charities or clubs. These not-for-profit organisations also need information. For example, a charity might like to know the differing sources of donations, or a club might like to know who still owes the annual subscription.

PART 1

Basic concepts of book-keeping

CHAPTER 1

What is book-keeping?

Welcome to the world of book-keeping! In this chapter you'll discover the basic purposes of book-keeping, get to grips with the fundamental terms and understand the importance of good, regular book-keeping in your business or organisation.

Basic purpose

Book-keeping is an important part of what is called the 'accounting cycle'. This cycle is a repetitive set of tasks performed during each accounting

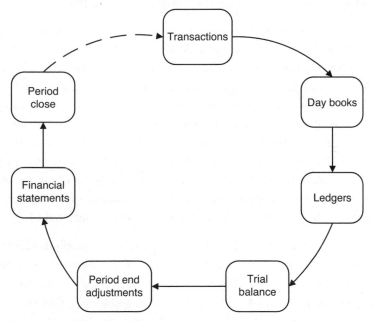

Figure 1.1 The accounting cycle

period – where a period could be one month, a quarter, six months, a year or any other timeframe. Figure 1.1 shows the elements of the accounting cycle.

The cycle starts with a business transaction, i.e. a sale, a purchase, a payment, etc. These transactions are captured in what traditionally are called 'day books'. This term refers to a time when all transactions would have been recorded on a daily basis in bound 'books' of some format. Such books are still used nowadays by many small businesses, but in most cases day books are replaced by some form of software. Next, the day books are summarised and the totals transferred to ledgers. Chapter 8 will give more detail on what a ledger is, but for now, suffice to say it is another 'book' that summarises the day books and incorporates other accounting entries called 'journals'. From the ledger, a summarised list of all account balances is produced – this is called the trial balance (see Chapter 8). The trial balance, with some adjustments, is the basis for the preparation of important accounting reports (see Chapter 9). The profit and loss account (or income statement) tells how much profit a business made (or how much it lost), whereas a balance sheet lists the assets, liabilities and capital of a business (see later in this chapter). Then the cycle starts all over again in the following accounting period.

Depending on the particular business or organisation, book-keeping may be performed to varying levels of difficulty. However, no matter what way book-keeping is done, it is clear from the accounting cycle shown in Figure 1.1 that book-keeping is a very important part of the full cycle. It often reminds me of the 'garbage in, garbage out' phrase used in computing. In other words, if you keep 'bad' books, how can you get any useful information on, for example, how much money was made or what the costs were? If you're self-employed, or perhaps keeping the books for your local tennis club, the one thing you will need is knowledge on how successful the organisation is, e.g. making profits in the business, or raising funds in the tennis club. Without book-keeping this simply is not possible.

Let's think of some examples of the varying levels of book-keeping in businesses. Traditionally, a small business might record transactions in the day books and perhaps keep a ledger. Then, once a year, the owner would go to an accountant with the day books and ledger. The accountant would then prepare a trial balance and the accounts/financial statements from these. A sole trader (see Chapter 2), who is a 'one-man-show', might not have the time or expertise even to keep day books, instead visiting an accountant more regularly to do the book-keeping. A large company (see Chapter 2) typically might complete a full accounting cycle itself, with its own accountants on the payroll.

No matter how simple or complex the organisation, the quality of accounting reports depends to a great extent on the data captured by the book-keeping processes. Of course nowadays, almost all book-keeping and accounting tasks use accounting software. In later chapters, you'll be introduced to one such piece of software. Accounting software offers great advantages, one being that all aspects of the accounting cycle are catered for. However, before we start to understand book-keeping, manual or computerised, there are some key terms to familiarise yourself with.

Some key terms

Like any trade or profession, there are terms in book-keeping that must be well understood before getting on with it. Some of the more important ones are given here, with more terms detailed later as the book progresses. The terms listed here are probably the most important ones to know and understand before you attempt any book-keeping tasks.

 brilliant definition

An *asset* is something that is owned or something to which you have rights, that will deliver a benefit, and for which costs can be readily determined.

Looking at this definition, it's easy to think of the assets we have in our personal life, e.g. a house, car or computer. Sticking with the house example, you might own your house if you're lucky enough to have paid off the mortgage. But even if you haven't paid off the mortgage, you still get a benefit and the house is considered a personal asset. And it is relatively easy to put a value (i.e. cost) on a house – for example, what you paid for it or what you could sell it for. However, there may be things about a house that a value cannot be put on. For example, you often hear of people who just won't sell a house as they're too fond of the view from their living room window.

Now, let's consider an example of a business asset. Let's assume you start up a business as a delivery service. You don't have enough money to buy a delivery van, so you lease it. This van lets you make deliveries and earn some money, i.e. you receive a benefit from the use of the van. So even though you don't have legal ownership of the van (as it's leased), it would be classified as an asset of the business. Of course, if you bought it outright, it would also be an asset.

if something can be classified as an asset it will be recorded in the books

For book-keeping purposes, if something can be classified as an asset, as per the definition above, it will be recorded in the books. If not, it is not recorded. For example, a business may consider the goodwill of its customers an asset, but this is something that cannot be valued reliably.

 brilliant definition

A *liability* is anything that is owed to someone else.

Most of us will have personal liabilities too, e.g. a balance on a home mortgage, a credit card bill, or a bank overdraft. Businesses too have liabilities. For example, if you buy goods from a supplier, you might not have to pay for 30 days. This debt would be a liability. Like assets, it must be possible to put a value on a liability; otherwise it would not be recorded in the books.

 brilliant definition

Capital is the money invested in a business by its owners.

The make-up of capital depends on the type of business. In a sole trader or partnership, capital is the money personally invested in the business by the owner(s). If a business is a limited company, then capital consists of the value of shares bought by shareholders of the company. Chapter 2 explains business types in more detail. Profits made in business after the initial investment by the owners is also included in capital.

brilliant definition

Income is the money received from the sale of goods or services.

Thus, income normally refers to monies received from customers, i.e. sales of a business. It might also include things like bank interest or income from investments made by a business.

 brilliant definition

Expenditure is cost incurred in the operating of a business.

Expenditure includes all costs in making/delivering the product/service of a business, e.g. purchases of goods for resale, materials, wages, heating, telephone, bank interest, accountants' fees, etc. One of the key points about expenditure is that it must be for the business only. For example, a repair to a business photocopier is an expense, whereas a repair to the owner's personal car would not be an expense. As you might be thinking, the list of business expenses might be endless, so they are normally grouped or classified. Chapter 9 will provide more detail on how business expenses are classified and summarised in the profit and loss account.

Some other terms

The following terms are also useful to know at this stage. More detail will be given in the relevant chapters later.

Credit sales/purchases

Buying or selling goods/services on credit means that payment will be made at a later date. Most businesses give credit to customers and take credit from suppliers.

Profit/loss

A profit is when income exceeds expenditure, a loss is the opposite.

When all the book-keeping is done, one of the outputs is a profit and loss account, which is also called the income statement.

Accounting period

This is the time period for which the accounts (or financial statements) are prepared. This may be a month, quarter, year or any other period as required by a business. Businesses will also have an accounting year-end, which often coincides with the calendar year, i.e. the accounting year-end is 31 December. For businesses that don't prepare financial statements more often, the year-end might be the only time they do so to calculate profits and work out any taxes owing.

Trade receivables

Trade receivables refer to the total amount of money owed to a business by its customers. The terms 'debtors' and 'accounts receivable' are also commonly used.

Trade payables

Trade payables refer to the total amount of money owed by a business to its suppliers. The terms 'creditors' and 'accounts payable' are also used.

Inventory

This is the amount of goods for resale a business holds in stock at any point in time. The term 'stock' is also often used, and is the one I prefer. Stock is usually tracked in great detail, with every movement recorded, e.g. each sale to a customer, each purchase from a supplier. Chapter 7 will give more detail on dealing with and valuing stock. Not every business will have stock on hand, e.g. service-type businesses.

Why bother with book-keeping?

While I haven't yet delved into nitty-gritty detail, looking back at Figure 1.1 it's easy to understand how important book-keeping is. You might be thinking, if it's so important, I don't want to make a mess so I'll just pay someone else to do it. Paying a book-keeper is fine once you have the resources to do so. If not, then your choice is not to bother at all and just get on with your business, or do the book-keeping yourself. No matter who does the book-keeping, the advantages of keeping good, accurate and timely records are too crucial to ignore. Now let's see why book-keeping is so important.

the advantages of keeping good, accurate and timely records are too crucial to ignore

 **brilliant** tip

Don't be afraid to hold up your hands and admit you don't have enough time to dedicate to doing all the book-keeping yourself. The worst thing you can do is ignore recording your business transactions.

Keeping track of sales

Any business wants to know how well sales are going. Sales drive the rest of the business – without ample sales you're in trouble. A business will also find it useful to identify sales trends, new markets, etc. regularly. Without proper and timely recording of every sale none of this would be possible. Think of amazon.com. Each time you buy a book, the sale is recorded and, over time, your purchases are used to make recommendations of other books you might like. Of course, amazon.com is highly automated, but it's a great example of how sales information can be used. Chapter 3 will deal with recording and keeping track of sales.

Keeping track of costs

Watching costs is just as important as generating sales. The only way to track costs over time is of course to record and analyse them. This means capturing all purchases of goods and expenses and summarising them in a useful way. For example, a business might want to compare its wage cost with a previous year or month. Additionally, if income and costs are recorded regularly, then it's also possible to calculate a profit or loss. The best advice to any business would be to *always* monitor and control costs. This helps the business to survive and prosper in the longer term. Chapters 4, 5, 6, 8 and 9 provide more detail on how to record various costs.

Checking your bank balance

In Chapter 5, you'll see how to record receipts and payments of a business. These may or may not be the same as the sales and purchases, as goods can be bought and sold on credit.

Let's assume all receipts and payments go through a business bank account. Each transaction will be recorded as it occurs, so any business should be able to determine the balance it has in the bank. You'd imagine there would be no difference between the balance a business says it has in the bank and what the bank says it has. But you'd be wrong. There are two main reasons for this. First, there may be book-keeping errors, e.g. a cheque for £190 was recorded in the books as £910. Such errors would cause a difference. Second, there may be items that have not yet been cleared by the bank and/or items entered on the account by the bank but not by the business. For example, a business might write a cheque to a supplier that has not yet lodged it in the bank. This 'uncleared' cheque would cause a difference. Another example would be bank interest or charges that have been charged to the account but not yet recorded in the books. This whole process of checking the bank balance is called 'bank reconciliation' and is dealt with in Chapter 5. For now, it is clear that making any comparison between the books and the bank is not possible without proper book-keeping in the first place. Also, this process is a check on the accuracy of the book-keeping of the business as all figures can be verified by comparison with the bank's records.

Reporting

the reporting of accounting information is impossible without good book-keeping

The reporting of accounting information is impossible without good book-keeping. Reports on sales, costs or other aspects of the business just would not be possible. An introduction to the profit and loss account (income statement) and the balance sheet is given in Chapter 9. These two reports are very important and are typically prepared at least once per year at the end of the accounting year. The profit and loss account summarises the income and expenditures of a business, while the balance sheet summarises assets, liabilities and capital. Most accounting software can prepare a profit and loss account and balance sheet at the click of a mouse, but their usefulness and accuracy are determined by the underlying book-keeping.

Paying taxes

Businesses pay taxes on the profits they make. Thus, without proper records, it's impossible to work out taxes owing. None of us likes to pay tax, but it gets a whole lot more costly if a business does not keep good records and pay the correct amount of tax on its profits.

In addition, as you'll see from Chapter 3 onwards, most businesses also have to account for VAT (value added tax). Without going into detail here, a business is more or less a tax collector for VAT. This means it must separately record any VAT on its transactions and pay it over to the tax authorities on a regular basis. Again, without good book-keeping practices, a business might run into trouble if recording VAT is not done well.

Final words

Now that you have some idea of what book-keeping entails, Chapter 2 gives some good tips before you get working. Given that book-keeping is so important in the accounting and business world, it does pay to stop and think before you act.

 brilliant recap

- Book-keeping is an important component of the accounting cycle.
- Its primary purpose is the recording of business transactions.
- Key terms to understand are: asset, liability, capital, income and expenditure.
- Book-keeping allows a business to: track sales, manage costs, report profits and calculate taxes.

CHAPTER 2

Before you start – some ideas and concepts

n this chapter you'll be introduced to some things you need to think about before you dive into recording business transactions. You'll learn some fundamental concepts from the world of accounting, which you need to know, and the various formats a business can have.

Some things to think about

What transactions need to be recorded and in how much detail?

The simple answer to this is: all transactions that fall within the accounting period (see Chapter 1) you're working on. In practice, this might mean waiting until all bills arrive, for example. At some point though, you will have to say that's it and put any 'late' items into the next month.

What is more important is the level of detail you want to capture. A great example of how business data captured can be extended to be extremely useful is the use of loyalty cards by supermarkets. By now, Tesco probably knows that I buy ice cream and wine most Fridays. They know this as I always scan my loyalty card, which connects the simple sale transaction to my personal details. Therefore, a business like Tesco can quite quickly tell what the average thirty-something buys on a Friday night. They can, and do, use such information to help stock their stores and get the right products for a particular store.

While perhaps an extravagant example, the use of loyalty cards shows how a business can capture information on transactions that really can drive how a business works. Before you sit down to start your book-keeping, have a think about how capturing the right data might help you match the future needs of customers, for example. Of course you still need to capture the basic data (such as the money value of each sale), but remember it is very hard to capture additional useful information once a transaction has passed.

 **example**

Most garages will record a car's registration number each time it visits for repair or service. The registration will appear on the customer's bill, but this also allows the garage to track the service and repair history of a car over time.

How should I summarise and report information?

How you do your book-keeping will impact on how you can summarise and report information. For example, if you sell two products but don't capture sales of each product, you'll never know how much of each you sold. In turn, you'd be unable to work out if one product is more profitable than the other.

In accounting, business transactions are recorded and summarised according to a 'chart of accounts'. For now, think of an account as a 'bucket' where similar transactions are collected. For example, there will be a bank account, where all cash is lodged and cheques are paid from. Or, a stationery account, where items like pens and paper will be recorded. A chart of accounts is simply a list of these accounts. Normally, accounts are assigned a code (perhaps a number) but this need not be so. Each account will be of a certain type, usually one of the following: asset, liability, capital, income or expense. Figure 2.1 shows a sample chart of accounts for a building contractor. You can see there are accounts for things like subcontractors, which is what you would expect in a construction business. The chart of accounts will vary by business, but there are normally a number of common items no matter what the business, e.g. wages.

	RC Builders	
6:03 PM 23/06/09	Account listing 23 June 2009	

Account	Type	Description
Bank account	Bank	
Construction in Progress	Other Current Asset	Costs for jobs in progress
Computer Equipment	Fixed Asset	Cost of computers
Computer Equipment:Cost	Fixed Asset	Cost of computers
Computer Equipment:Depreciation	Fixed Asset	Depreciation of computers
Construction Equipment	Fixed Asset	Equipment used in the construction process
Furniture and Fixtures:Cost	Fixed Asset	Cost of furniture and fixtures
Furniture and Fixtures:Depreciation	Fixed Asset	Depreciation of furniture and fixtures
Land	Fixed Asset	Land owned by the company
Motor Vehicles:Cost	Fixed Asset	Business cars and trucks, registered in the name of the business
Motor Vehicles:Depreciation	Fixed Asset	Depreciation on company cars and trucks, registered in the name of the business
Office Equipment:Cost	Fixed Asset	Office equipment including printers, photocopiers
Office Equipment:Depreciation	Fixed Asset	Depreciation on company-owned office equipment including photocopiers, etc.
Vehicles	Fixed Asset	Business automobiles and trucks, registered in the name of the business
Security Deposits Asset	Other Asset	Deposits and other returnable funds held by other entities (Rent, Utilities, etc.)
Accounts Payable	Accounts Payable	Amounts owed to suppliers
Construction Loans	Other Current Liability	Draws on construction loans
Payroll Liabilities	Other Current Liability	Employee-related payroll liabilities
VAT Liability	Other Current Liability	
Owner's Drawings	Equity	Monies taken out of the business by the owner
Owner's Equity	Equity	Monies invested in the business by the owner, and profits kept in company accounts
Construction Income	Income	Income received from customers for construction jobs
Rental Income	Income	Rental Income
Blueprints and Reproduction	Cost of Goods Sold	Blueprints, photostats, and other printing expenses
Bond Expense	Cost of Goods Sold	Construction bonds expenses directly related to jobs
Construction Materials Costs	Cost of Goods Sold	Construction materials costs
Equipment Rental for Jobs	Cost of Goods Sold	Rent paid for rented equipment used on jobs
Other Construction Costs	Cost of Goods Sold	Other costs directly related to jobs such as waste disposal, onsite storage rental, etc.
Subcontractors Expense	Cost of Goods Sold	Subcontracted services performed by other contractors
Tools and Small Equipment	Cost of Goods Sold	Purchases of tools or small equipment used on jobs
Worker's Compensation Insurance	Cost of Goods Sold	Worker's compensation insurance premiums
Advertising and Promotion	Expense	Advertising, marketing, graphic design, and other promotional expenses
Motor expenses	Expense	Fuel, oil, repairs, and other maintenance for business cars and trucks
Bank Service Charges	Expense	Bank account service fees, bad cheque charges and other bank fees
Business Licences and Permits	Expense	Business licences, permits, and other business-related fees
Charitable Donations	Expense	Contributions to qualifying charitable organisations
Computer and Internet Expenses	Expense	Computer supplies, off-the-shelf software, online fees, and other computer or internet-related expenses
Depreciation Expenses	Expense	Depreciation on equipment, buildings and improvements
Dues and Subscriptions	Expense	Subscriptions and membership dues for civic, service, professional, trade organisations
Insurance Expenses	Expense	Insurance expenses
Interest Expenses	Expense	Interest payments on business loans, credit card balances, or other business debt
Meals and Entertainment	Expense	Business meals and entertainment expenses, including travel-related meals (may have limited deductibility)
Miscellaneous Expenses	Expense	Miscellaneous expenses not categorised elsewhere. Use memo field to describe business purpose
Office Expenses	Expense	Office Expenses
Payroll Expenses	Expense	Employee-related payroll expenses
Postage and Delivery	Expense	Postage, courier and pick-up and delivery services
Professional Fees	Expense	Payments to accounting professionals and attorneys for accounting or legal services
Rent and Rates	Expense	Rent and rates paid in the business
Repairs and Maintenance	Expense	Incidental repairs and maintenance of business assets that do not add to the value or appreciably prolong its life
Repairs to buildings	Expense	Incidental repairs and maintenance of business assets that do not add to the value or appreciably prolong its life
Repairs to Plant and Machinery	Expense	Incidental repairs and maintenance of business assets that do not add to the value or appreciably prolong its life
Staff Training	Expense	Seminars, educational expenses and employee development, not including travel
Taxes	Expense	Tax Charge
Telephone	Expense	Telephone and long-distance charges, faxing, and other fees. Not equipment purchases
Travelling and Entertainment	Expense	Business-related travel expenses including airline tickets, taxi fares, hotel and other travel expenses
Uniforms	Expense	Uniforms for employees and contractors
Utilities	Expense	Water, gas and electricity expenses

Figure 2.1 Sample chart of accounts

As you can see in Figure 2.1, each account has a name, type and description. The account type is useful, as it defines the financial statement to which the account belongs (see Chapter 9).

As I'll show in later chapters, the data recorded by the book-keeper makes its way into an account, such as those already mentioned, and then to the financial statements.

the data recorded by the book-keeper makes its way into an account, and then to the financial statements

Can I do my book-keeping manually or should I use a computer?

Despite what we have been told probably for 30 years now, the paperless office seems elusive. Yes, computers and computer software are wonderful, but you should use software only when it (1) does what we want it to do and (2) delivers a benefit beyond what we currently do.

In book-keeping and accounting, it is still quite common for small businesses to keep manual records. These typically are kept in a hardback book, journal or diary of some kind and organised by transaction type, e.g. sales, purchases, payments, etc. If a business has a low volume of transactions, manual records are often just fine. In fact, when I teach book-keeping, I always start off showing how to do things manually. This is what you'll learn from Chapter 3 onwards. But, as you might guess, as businesses get larger, manual book-keeping is just not good enough. This is not because it's faulty in any way. Rather it's because a business requires more detailed information from its accounting data to make quick and fast business decisions.

Looking back at the accounting cycle in Chapter 1, accounting software covers all steps once the transaction has been recorded in the software. Therefore, information on costs, for example, is available instantly. This simply is not possible when done manually. You'll see what I mean when we get down to doing stuff from Chapter 3 onwards. Also, software is relatively cheap, ranging from about £10 on eBay to £60 for entry-level software from more well-known companies like Sage, TAS and QuickBooks.

The decision to use software is often best made as soon as a business is up and running. But, if requirements are simple, software might be a waste of time. For example, a local community association formed to preserve the village post office is unlikely to have complex requirements – just simply knowing how much money has been raised and spent might be enough.

Every business is different of course, and a lot depends upon the plans of the owners. Good advice would be to use software from the outset once you are comfortable with the basic concepts of book-keeping and with using a computer. It can be difficult to assess which software is best for you, so the sensible thing to do is ask an accountant for help. As a minimum, though, any software must be able to keep track of all transactions dealt with in this book, and produce standard accounting reports. My favourite accounting software is QuickBooks, which I'll show you in later chapters.

brilliant tip

Look on the internet for comparisons of the features of various accounting software packages. Don't go overboard on fancy software features you might never use – just keep it simple to begin with.

Should I get help?

It is easy to be put off by lots of numbers, books, software, etc. A lot of business people are just not that interested in doing the 'hard' work of book-keeping. However, if you are to employ a book-keeper or accountant to do the work for you, it helps to know what the job involves. Otherwise, you might find yourself with an employee who is not skilled enough or an accountant who is overcharging for the work done. At least by reading the rest of this book you'll either have a good knowledge of how to do the book-keeping yourself or, alternatively, will be sure that it is being done in a reasonable manner by someone else.

Don't be afraid to ask for help or guidance. It's always better to seek help than continue to do things wrong. Remember just how important book-keeping is in the accounting cycle – it determines the accuracy of all later accounting information and this information is used to make crucial business decisions.

book-keeping determines the accuracy of all later accounting information used to make crucial business decisions

Some fundamental accounting concepts

There are some concepts in the accounting world with which you need to be familiar before you start book-keeping tasks. These are not difficult to grasp, but are crucial knowledge.

The accounting entity

In accounting, any business is regarded as a separate entity. Here's an example. Assume you are a self-employed van courier. Your delivery van breaks down so you get a mechanic to repair it. Your personal car is not running too well, belching out black smoke from time to time. So you get the mechanic to have a look at your car too. The mechanic repairs both your van and the car. He gives you one bill for both repairs. Is the repair of the car an expense of your business? You might have guessed no, and you are correct. This is because the expense of the car repair is not for the business. Thus, there is a difference between the business entity and your personal items (like your car). Only the van is regarded as part of the business entity and, thus, only the cost of the repair to the van should be recorded as an expense. The cost of the car repair could be recorded as a 'drawing' from the business, which you'll learn more about in later chapters.

The accruals concept

The accruals (or matching) concept is fundamental to the book-keeping and accounting of any business entity. It simply means that income and expenditure are recorded when a transaction occurs or is related to, not when cash is paid or received for the transaction.

 **brilliant** example

Assume a business prepares accounts to 31 December each year. A bill is received from a supplier on 5 January of the following year and this bill is paid on 20 January. The bill relates to goods delivered in December. So, under the accruals concept, the cost of these goods is recorded in the books in the month of December. It doesn't matter when the bill is actually paid. Thus, the accounts to 31 December will show a liability for the unpaid bill.

In a similar way to the above example, let's assume an insurance bill is paid on 1 October. This bill covers the business insurance for one year from that date. Should the full cost be in the accounts to 31 December? If you said no, you're right. In this example, three months (1 October–31 December) relates to the current year and nine months to the next year.

Thus, three months (or 25 per cent) of the cost would appear in the current year's accounts. The remaining (75 per cent) is termed a prepayment and is classified as an asset. So, the accruals concept says that transactions are recorded as they occur, not when cash is paid or received.

Accounting on the basis of cash paid and received is allowed in some cases for small businesses and I'll provide some more detail on this in Chapter 3.

Going concern concept

This concept means that accounts are prepared under the assumption that a business will continue to operate for the foreseeable future. This is normally the case. If, however, the business discontinues, or is likely to, the value of some items might be affected. For example, if customers owed money, they might be reluctant to pay, or perhaps the value of the business premises might be higher or lower than the value in the accounts.

Business formats

In a legal sense, a business can take many formats. It is important to understand these, as each may have different book-keeping and accounting requirements.

Sole trader

The simplest form of business is a 'sole trader'. This is your typical self-employed person, like an electrician, plumber or the delivery van driver mentioned in the earlier example. As a sole trader, you are the only person who benefits from the rewards of the business. On the downside, you may also suffer all losses. But remember the entity concept referred to earlier, and make sure that business and personal expenses, etc. are not confused.

Partnership

In a partnership two or more people form a business and share the rewards and risks. Partnerships are normally governed by a partnership agreement. This is a legally binding agreement which sets out what each partner does, what share of profit they are entitled to, what risks they cover, etc. Partnerships are quite common in professions like accounting, law and medicine. This is mainly because no one person will have all the skills needed to conduct the business successfully. Like a sole trader, each partner is entitled to a share of the profits or must bear losses.

Limited company

A business may also be a limited company. Unlike the previous two forms, the word 'limited' suggests that the owners are somehow protected. The owners of a company are called shareholders. Their liability is limited to the amount they have unpaid on shares they agreed to buy. So, if I agreed to buy £100 of shares and I paid only £60, no matter what happens to the company, my liability (or debt) is £40. In a sole trader or partnership, liability could be unlimited and, in an extreme situation, personal assets might be used to clear business debts. Limited companies can be either private or public. A private company cannot sell its shares to the general public, whereas a public company can (normally through a stock market).

Not-for-profit organisations

The previous three business formats are for-profit organisations. This means that they exist to make profits for their owners. Not-for-profit organisations are ones that might not have making a profit as an objective, but are nevertheless legally constituted. A typical example is a charity, such as Oxfam. In most countries, charities are well regulated and must keep records of income and expenditure in a manner very similar to a business. For example, The Charities Commission in the UK regulates the setting up of charities and monitors existing ones. However, once you know how to do book-keeping tasks in any for-profit organisation, the same principles can be applied in a not-for-profit organisation.

brilliant recap

- Before you start doing book-keeping, be clear on what needs to be recorded, in how much detail and how you summarise and report the information.

- You can use readily available computer software to help you.

- Ask for help if you need it. It's better to get things right.

- There are some accounting concepts to be learned: the accounting entity, accruals and going concern.

- Businesses can be sole traders, partnerships or limited companies. Most organisations are for-profit, but there are also not-for-profit organisations like charities.

PART 2

Doing the book-keeping

CHAPTER 3

Recording what you sell

I n this chapter you will learn how to record sales of a business. We'll start with the recording of sales for two reasons: (1) it is a nice easy introduction and (2) because income from sales is so important to any business.

Sales can refer to the sale of goods (e.g. a laptop) or the provision of a service (e.g. repairs to a laptop). I'll also introduce value added tax. First, we'll look at cash sales, then credit sales and finally some further sales-related transactions. In each section you'll be shown first how to record sales in a traditional manual format. Then, you'll be introduced to the QuickBooks accounting software for the first time, showing how sales are recorded.

Recording cash sales

Many businesses receive payment immediately for the goods or services they provide. Some examples would be newsagents, doctors' practices and fast-food outlets. When a sale is made and payment received at the same time, this is referred to as a cash sale.

You might think of cash sales as those where notes and coins are exchanged, but of course cash sales include many other payment forms, e.g. debit cards, credit cards, PayPal and any other electronic payment format. Regardless of the payment format, cash sales are usually lodged on a regular basis to the business bank account.

In book-keeping terms, for most businesses a cash sale means making sure the sale is recorded and that a receipt is given to the customer for the cash received. Cash sales are often recorded using a cash register of some kind. In most large retail stores, for example, you'll see that barcode scanners are linked to cash registers and automatically record the sale, whereas in some smaller stores, the operator usually has to key in a sale.

 **brilliant** tip

> Always issue a receipt for a cash sale. It is a record of the cash received and provides the customer with proof of purchase.

ideally, there should be two copies of the receipt, one for the business and one for the customer

Some small businesses may not have a cash register, or the volume of cash sales is quite small. If this is the case, a handwritten receipt can be used. Ideally, there should be two copies of the receipt, one for the business and one for the customer. Figure 3.1 shows an example of such a receipt.

SALE RECEIPT			NO. 346	
Customer: John Taylor, 51 Park St, Southend		Fred's Fax & Copy Centre, 40 High St, Northend		
DATE	**DESCRIPTION**			**AMOUNT**
23 July 2010	Binding of promotional brochures 10 reams of A4 paper			£50.00 £20.00
			SUBTOTAL	£70.00
			VAT	£12.25
			TOTAL	£82.25

Figure 3.1 Sample sale receipt

Whether a receipt is handwritten or printed from a cash register it contains a lot of useful information for book-keepers. Looking at Figure 3.1 you can see why. The amount of cash collected is shown, the type of products sold, the quantity sold, and the VAT charged. A receipt printed from a cash register would contain similar details. The difference with an automated system such as a cash register is that the sales for the day are usually summarised automatically – no need for a calculator to tot up all receipts. Each sale could also be used to reduce the amount of goods in stock (see Chapter 7), a task that is easily done once you have some form of automated system. Total cash sales for a day are recorded in the cash book, which you'll learn about in Chapter 5. For now, you can see just how important it is to capture data when a sale is made.

You might ask, how can a business be sure all cash sales are recorded, particularly those for hard cash (notes and coins)? In a small business it's pretty easy to keep an eye on staff, less so in a large business. A simple policy of issuing a receipt for every sale is a good start. If a cash register is used, a daily printout of all sales can be produced and this should agree with the cash in the register drawer. If not, then there is an error or perhaps deliberate fraud – this is always a possibility when cash is present in any business. Some businesses, like pubs for example, adopt measures such as installing hidden cameras to monitor staff with access to cash. I don't think it is ever possible to be 100 per cent sure every sale of a business is captured, but if you're 99 per cent sure, that's good enough.

Introduction to VAT

In Figure 3.1, the receipt shows a VAT amount. VAT is short for value added tax. This is a tax that is added to most business transactions and it applies to most businesses. The current standard VAT rate in the UK is 17.5%, and any business with total sales of more than £68,000 (as from 1 May 2009) must register for and account for VAT. Other European countries have lower or higher rates, but the general concepts described here are the same in most countries. In addition to the standard rate, there is normally a reduced rate (5% in the UK), a zero rate and an exempt category. VAT is a complex area so don't be afraid to ask for help from an accountant. The basic knowledge you must have as a book-keeper is how much VAT to charge on the products or services you provide and how to record it.

 example

Examples of VAT rates applicable to products and services in the UK

Reduced rate (5%)

● Electricity for domestic and residential use.

● Gas for domestic and residential use.

- Heating oil for domestic and residential use.
- Solid fuel for domestic and residential use.
- Insulation (installation).
- Solar panels (installation).
- Altering an empty residential building.

Zero rate (0%)

- Building services for disabled people.
- Equipment for blind or partially sighted people.
- Food – but not meals in restaurants or hot takeaways.
- Books and newspapers.
- Children's clothes and shoes.
- Public transport.

Exempt[1]

- Insurance.
- Providing credit.
- Most services provided by doctors and dentists.
- Education and training, if certain conditions are met.
- Fundraising events by charities, if certain conditions are met.
- Membership subscriptions.

[1] Exempt means that the VAT laws say that an activity is exempt from the VAT rules.

Source: www.hmrc.gov.uk/vat/start/introduction.htm

You will learn about VAT in more detail in this chapter and in Chapter 4. Now you know that a business normally adds VAT to the price of its products or services. As a consumer, we may not always see VAT on a receipt we get, but generally it is there.

Recording credit sales

A credit sale is when goods or services are provided to a customer with payment deferred until a later date. As with a cash sale, a customer will be given some proof of the sale transaction. This document is called a sales invoice. Figure 3.2 shows an example of a hand-written invoice, which is often used by smaller businesses. Accounting software can also produce invoices, which you'll see later in this chapter.

SALE RECEIPT		NO. 143
Customer: Terry Money	Money Solutions, Farmhouse, Essex	
DATE	**DESCRIPTION**	**AMOUNT**
12 August 2007	To purchase a new computer To set up and supply software	£1750 £250
	SALE TOTAL	£2000
	VAT @ 17.5%	£350
	TOTAL	£2350

Figure 3.2 Sample sales invoice

As you can see, a sales invoice is not too unlike a receipt. The difference is that no cash has been received when the sale is made. Therefore, this means the book-keeper now has the job of keeping track of which sales invoices are paid and unpaid on top of recording the sale. Let's deal first with recording the sale.

In a manual book-keeping system, credit sales are recorded in a book called the *sales day book*. This is simply a book (or maybe a spreadsheet) that records some details from each sales invoice. Typically it is presented in a columnar format as shown in Figure 3.3.

Great Garages

Sales day book

Date	Customer	Ref.	Total	Sales 5%	Sales 17.5%	VAT
01/10/2009	Great Doors Ltd	134	1,050.00	1000.00		50.00
01/10/2009	John Adams	135	352.50		300.00	52.50
03/10/2009	Steve Grey	136	1,175.00		1,000.00	175.00
05/10/2009	Great Doors Ltd	137	1,645.00		1,400.00	245.00
06/10/2009	Great Doors Ltd	138	2,350.00		2,000.00	350.00
15/10/2009	Littlewoods	139	2,749.50		2,340.00	409.50
16/10/2009	Martin King	140	47.00		40.00	7.00
17/10/2009	Judy Talbot	141	63.00	60.00		3.00
30/10/2009	Great Doors Ltd	142	352.50		300.00	52.50
			9,784.50	1,060.00	7,380.00	1,344.50

Figure 3.3 Sample sales day book

This sales day book shows how the sales invoices of a business called Great Garages might be recorded. What I have shown is the most basic level of information. By the way, I have also used a spreadsheet so I don't have to add the numbers manually. You can see that sales are at different VAT rates, as indicated by the two columns labelled 'Sales'. The VAT amount is shown in the far right column, with the column to the left showing the total for each sale. VAT needs to be separated as the VAT amount is paid to the tax authorities later. The total amount sold at each VAT rate also needs to be reported to the tax authorities, hence the two columns recording sales at different VAT rates. Finally, the 'Ref' column refers to the sales invoice number and can be used to trace back from the sales day book to the specific invoice.

 brilliant definition

Gross sales refer to the amount of sales including VAT. Net sales refer to sales excluding VAT.

You could of course choose to record your sales data in much more detail. For example, you could have one column for sales of goods, another for services or even multiple columns for each product. This becomes very tricky in a manual book-keeping system and here's where accounting software can really help.

 brilliant tip

When you total any day book (we'll see more in later chapters), always make sure the sum of all analysis columns, i.e. all columns other than the 'total' column, equals the total of the 'total' column. This is referred to as 'checking the cross-tots' and is very important.

The data recorded in the sales day book is used for two things. First, the totals are recorded further in ledger accounts (see Chapter 8) which are used to prepare accounting reports. Second, the individual sales transactions are recorded in personal accounts in order to keep track of balances owed. For example, in Figure 3.3 there are four separate sales to Great Doors Ltd. These amounts would be recorded in an account for Great Doors Ltd, showing a total amount owing of £5,397.50. It might sound confusing at this stage that there are two ledgers, but this is how accounting is structured. One ledger is used to keep track of individual personal accounts of suppliers and customers. This is often called the *personal ledger*. Personal ledgers are used quite frequently by book-keepers. The other ledger is used to track all aspects of a business, i.e. all assets, liabilities, capital, revenue and expenses. This ledger is called the *nominal ledger* and tends to be used more by accountants. You'll get more detail in Chapter 8.

You might ask why a business would want to sell on credit. The simple answer is that this is a more flexible approach to selling and will attract more customers. You do need to be careful to whom credit is granted though.

> credit is a more flexible approach to selling and will attract more customers

brilliant tip

Before granting credit to a customer:

- check their credit history and/or ask for references from other businesses they deal with
- use a credit rating agency to assess customers – there is normally a fee for this
- set a limit on the amount of credit given
- follow up with reminders or phone calls when payment is due.

Granting credit is a trade-off between not getting paid and losing a sale. If you don't grant credit at all, or for long enough, customers will go elsewhere. A good thing to do is have a look around to see how other businesses similar to yours grant credit. Whatever you decide on, the most important thing to do is to apply the policy you set. For example, if you decide to grant 30 days' credit to a customer and 40 days later you have not had payment, get on the phone and request payment. If payment is not forthcoming, you could stop the customer buying more until the debt is paid.

Recording sales in QuickBooks®

Now that you know the basics of recording sales in a manual system, let's see what QuickBooks can do. QuickBooks is one of a number of readily available accounting software packages. Others include TAS, Sage and MYOB. The examples used in this book are from QuickBooks Professional 2008, which costs about £350. There are other versions of QuickBooks which are less and more expensive, depending on the functionality offered.

Recording cash sales in QuickBooks

Recording a cash sale in QuickBooks is very much like writing a receipt, as shown earlier. Take a look at the screenshot from QuickBooks in Figure 3.4.

In Figure 3.4, you can see the items sold clearly, to whom the sale was made, when, the value of the sale and the VAT amount. You'll also see that the cash was deposited to the business bank account (bottom left of the screenshot). That's it! The one major advantage of accounting software is that once a transaction is entered, such as this cash sale, all other associated book-keeping entries are made, i.e. the deposit to the bank is also recorded and all ledger accounts are updated.

Recording credit sales in QuickBooks

Recording a credit sale in QuickBooks is rather like writing out a sales invoice as shown in Figure 3.2. Figure 3.5 is another screenshot, showing a credit sale.

The most noticeable differences compared with the cash sale are that there is no deposit shown to a bank account and the terms of payment are shown. The terms are Net 30, which means the customer should pay the full amount owing in 30 days from the date of the invoice. Once a credit sale is entered in QuickBooks, it then prints out a sales invoice, which you can customise with your business logo, etc.

As already mentioned, sales such as this one, and those shown previously in the sales day book, are recorded in ledger accounts. In fact all business transactions are: sales, purchases, payments, etc. So as well as being recorded in a day book (or in a computer), all business transactions are

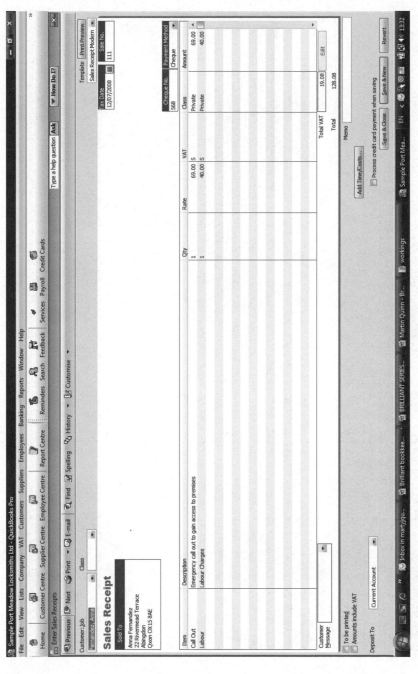

Figure 3.4 Cash sales in QuickBooks

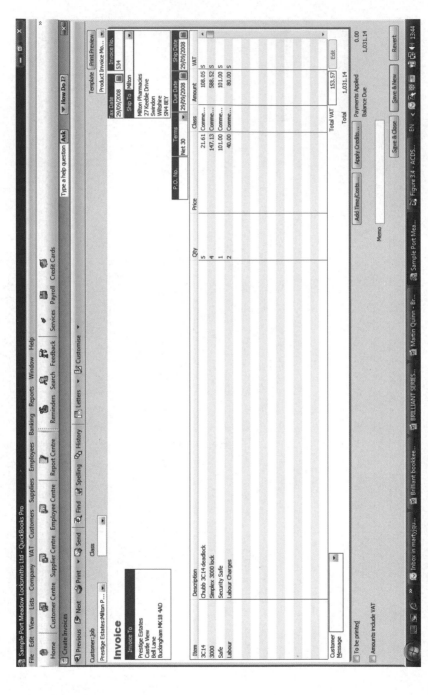

Figure 3.5 Credit sale invoice in QuickBooks

recorded in a ledger account (look back at Figure 1.1). From here on, I'll tell you which ledger accounts are used as business transactions occur, with greater details on ledger accounts in Chapter 8.

Ignoring VAT for a moment, when a cash sale occurs, two ledger accounts are affected – the sales account and the bank account. Both are increased as money goes into the bank and a new sale has been recorded. When a credit sale is made there are also two accounts involved. One is the sales account again, the other an account called trade receivables (sometimes called accounts receivables or debtors). Again, both are increased as a new sale has occurred and now a customer owes us more money. When there is VAT, then there are three accounts in both cases. A VAT account will be increased each time a sale is made as we are simply collecting the VAT for payment to the tax authorities at a later date.

Discounts and returns

Discounts

Many businesses offer discounts to customers from time to time. These are called *discounts allowed*. The normal aim of allowing a discount is to increase sales, but sometimes discounts might be given on old or damaged items.

It is normal to record any discounts given when a sale is made. This allows you to add up the cost of discounts and see if it is too costly. If you have to offer discounts a lot, in order to get sales, have a think about your pricing or have a close look at what competitors might do.

Recording a discount is simple. Whether in a manual sales day book or in QuickBooks, the amount of the discount is deducted from the net sale amount on the sales invoice. In a manual sales day book, you might want to include an additional column for discounts.

As you might have guessed by now, if a discount is given, a sale transaction now will be recorded in four different ledger accounts – there will be an increase in the sales account, the trade receivables account or bank account (depending on whether the sale is cash or credit), the VAT account and the discounts allowed account.

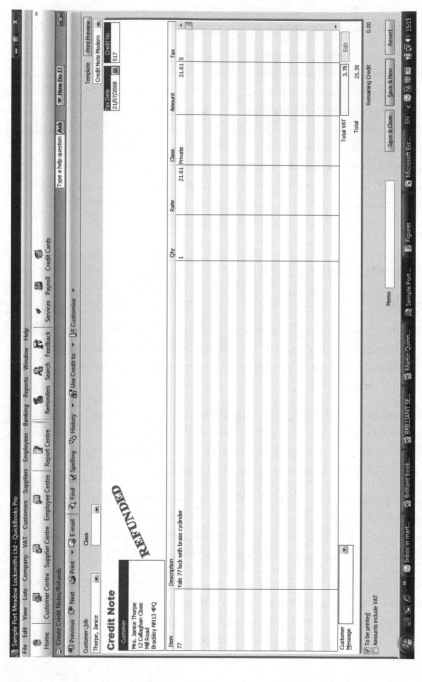

Figure 3.6 Sales credit note in QuickBooks

Returns

Sometimes customers are sold an incorrect or damaged product and they return it. Again, this should be recorded as it can allow you to assess the value of goods returned. You can then investigate why, if the returns amount is significant. It also reduces the amount owed by the customer. Most businesses have a policy on returns, for example stating that returns must be made within 21 days and goods must be in their original packaging.

Sales returns can be recorded in a separate day book, called the *sales returns day book*. This book is very similar to the sales day book shown in Figure 3.3. It is normal to issue a document called a *credit note* when a return occurs. This is similar to a sales invoice in layout and content. In QuickBooks, a credit note is recorded as shown in Figure 3.6.

In terms of ledger accounts, when a return occurs the transaction will be recorded in accounts similar to when a sale is made. The difference is that a sales return account will be increased, while the customer's account is decreased as they now owe us less money.

Monitoring trade receivables

One of the benefits of using accounting software like QuickBooks is that it is relatively easy to track how much customers owe you and for how long the money is owed. When you do sell on credit, probably the most important part of controlling credit is ensuring customers actually pay on time. In reality, very few customers will ever pay exactly on time and you will have to chase them.

> very few customers will ever pay exactly on time

A key tool to help you is a report called an aged receivables report. Figure 3.7 shows one such report from QuickBooks.

In this report, you can see that the amounts owed by each customer are shown in 30-day intervals. This is quite common in many accounting software packages. You can use the aged receivables report as a starting point to control the credit granted. For example, if you assume that the credit given to Business Security Ltd is granted for 60 days, then as the

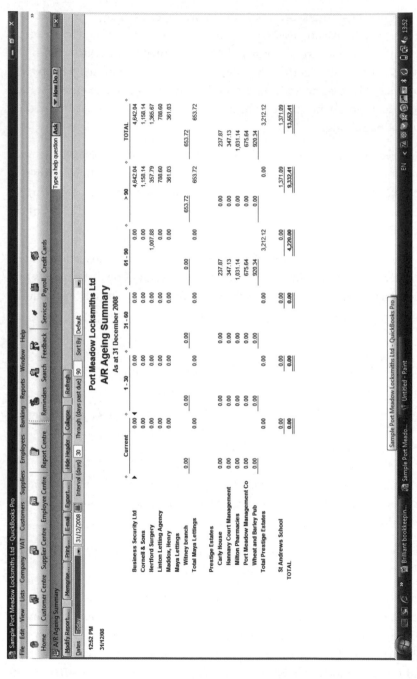

Figure 3.7 Aged receivables report in QuickBooks

full amount owed is older than 90 days, you need to start pursuing the customer for payment without delay.

 tip

> The age of an invoice starts from the invoice date. So, invoice without delay as to do otherwise effectively extends the credit period and the time taken to get paid. Once goods have been invoiced, adopt a systematic and regular approach to collecting money. Don't let amounts owed by customers get either too large or too old.

If your business has sales staff, it is a good idea to give them a copy of an aged receivables report as they visit customers. In extreme cases, sales staff can be blocked from taking new orders from customers who have large or old amounts outstanding.

 brilliant recap

- Cash sales are sales where payment is received immediately and include credit/debit card sales. Credit sales are sales that are paid for at a later date.
- Both cash and credit sales need to be recorded by a business. A receipt is usually issued for each cash sale, an invoice for each credit sale.
- Credit sales are recorded in a sales day book, cash sales in the cash book (see Chapter 5).
- A business may have to charge VAT on its sales.
- Every sale transaction is also recorded in the personal and nominal ledgers (see Chapter 8).
- Discounts and returns from customers can occur. These also are recorded.
- A customer's creditworthiness should be checked before any credit is granted.
- Customers need to be monitored to ensure they comply with credit terms given.

CHAPTER 4

Recording what you buy

Having looked at recording sales in Chapter 3, in this chapter you'll learn how a business records what it buys. Most businesses buy both goods and services in the course of making a product or delivering a service. These of course have to be recorded in order to compare with sales income to see if the business is profitable or not.

What a business buys can be broadly described as either *purchases* or *expenses*.

what a business buys can be broadly described as either purchases or expenses

 brilliant definition

Purchases refer to the cost of goods bought for resale or raw materials that are used to make a product. The cost includes transport, import duties and other costs to get the goods to the business. *Expenses* refer to all other costs of doing business.

In this chapter, you'll learn how credit purchases and small cash expenses are recorded. Chapter 5 deals with other types of expense.

Recording credit purchases

You'll see in Chapter 9 that the difference between total sales and total purchases for a period is called gross profit. Expenses such as wages, rent, heating and light are deducted from gross profit to see how much actual profit a business makes. Therefore, recording purchases accurately is very important. Of course some businesses do not have purchases in the sense we are referring to here. For example, a recruitment agency does not buy anything to resell or make into a product. The agency probably would still acquire items or services, which do need to be recorded.

In a manual book-keeping system, the *purchases day book* is traditionally used to record purchases of goods and services on credit. Even if a business does not have purchases for resale, or does not purchase raw materials to make something, it can still use a purchases day book to record items bought on credit. So the purchases day book is not purely for recording purchases in the sense defined above; it can be used to record expenses.

A purchases day book is quite similar in format to the sales day book shown in Chapter 3 (p. 35). Figure 4.1 shows an example of what a purchases day book might look like.

Great Garages

Purchases day book

Date		Ref.	Total	Purchases 5%	Purchases 17.5%	VAT
15/10/2009	Mark Hanley	300	525.00	500.00		25.00
16/10/2009	John's Parts	301	1,645.00		1,400.00	245.00
17/10/2009	Town Council – water charge	302	470.00		400.00	70.00
20/10/2009	AB Supplies Ltd	303	658.00		560.00	98.00
23/10/2009	MegaSupplies	304	8,225.00		7,000.00	1,225.00
25/10/2009	AB Supplies Ltd	305	235.00		200.00	35.00
29/10/2009	John's Parts	306	210.00	200.00		10.00
			11,968.00	700.00	9,560.00	1,708.00

Figure 4.1 Sample purchases day book

As you can see, the purchases day book is pretty much the same as the sales day book. Each purchase invoice from suppliers is identified and the net, VAT and total amounts are shown in separate columns. Figure 4.1 shows two VAT rates, but this might not always be so. The 'Ref.' column refers to a sequence number in a filing system, which makes it easy to locate the invoice. You can use any reference number once you understand what it means. I like to start at reference number '1' and put all purchase invoices in one file. You could also have a file for each supplier, but this tends to occupy a lot of shelf space.

This example might not be the best if a purchases day book is also used to record expenses. For example, if the business were to get an invoice for advertising, where would this go? You can add extra columns of course. Many small businesses I know have two more columns in their purchases day book for services (obtained on credit) at the standard and reduced VAT rates. This improves the usefulness of the information when it comes to recording it in the ledgers and preparing financial statements.

Once purchase invoices have been recorded, the purchases day book is used in a similar way to the sales day book. Each line from the day book is used to update the account of the supplier in the personal ledger. This increases the total amount owed to the particular supplier. The total of the net amount of the invoices from the purchases day book increases the purchases or expense account in the nominal ledger and the total VAT amount decreases the VAT account in the nominal ledger. In turn, this VAT is offset against the VAT collected from customers (see more in the final section of this chapter).

Now let's see how to record a credit purchase in QuickBooks. The term 'bill' is used instead of invoice in QuickBooks. Figure 4.2 shows how to enter a bill.

The screenshot in Figure 4.2 shows a simple bill from a utility company, i.e. this is an expense rather than a purchase for resale. In this example, a bill for £1,175 is being recorded, which is £1,000 plus £175 VAT. The top portion of the screen shows the supplier's name, the date of the invoice, the total and the credit terms: Net 7, which means due in 7 days with no discount available. The lower portion of the screen shows how this expense is to be recorded in the nominal ledger. In this case, the invoice will be recorded in an account called 'Utilities'. The net amount (£1,000) is recorded to this account. The VAT amount of £175 is also shown and this will be recorded in the VAT account.

When a purchase invoice is recorded in QuickBooks you can select whether it is for an expense (see the encircled tab in Figure 4.2) or a purchase. QuickBooks refers to purchase of goods as purchase of 'items' (see the encircled tab in Figure 4.3).

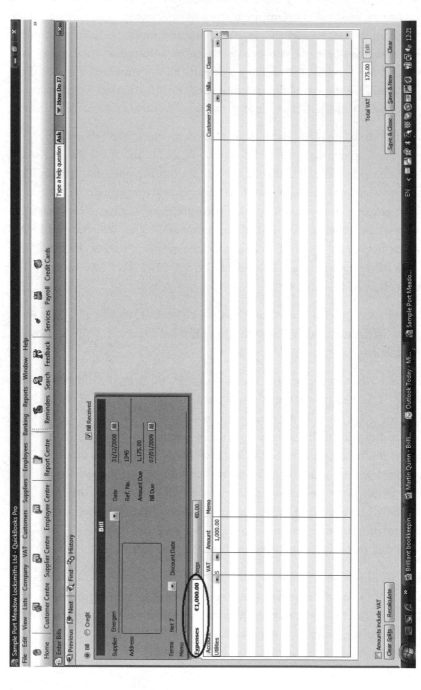

Figure 4.2 Recording a credit purchase in QuickBooks

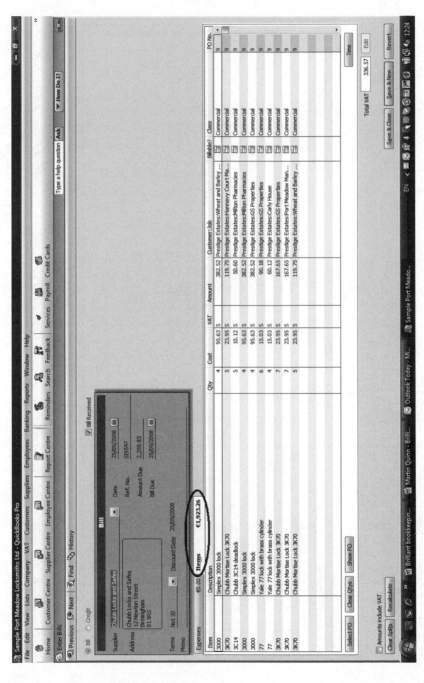

Figure 4.3 Analysing a purchase of 'items' in QuickBooks

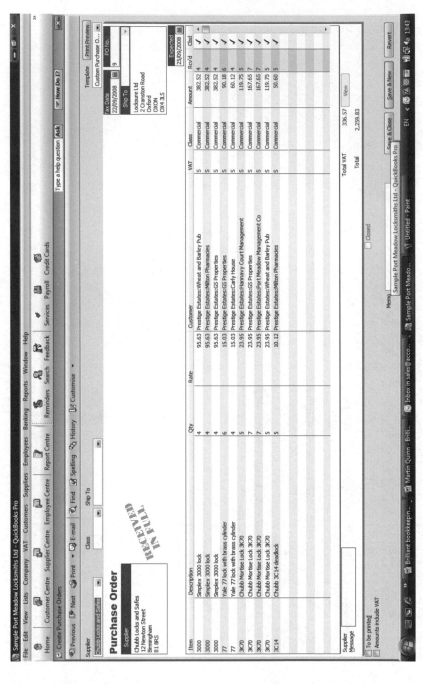

Figure 4.4 A purchase order in QuickBooks

Here we can see a lot more, particularly in the bottom portion of the screen. What we see is a detailed list of all items purchased – a description of each item, the quantity bought, the unit and total price and the VAT amount. Recording each purchase at this level of detail not only captures the cost of the purchase but also records the quantity of each item so that the number in stock can be updated. This stock amount is, in turn, reduced by selling these items.

This is an example of where accounting software has some clear advantages over manually maintained records. If you look at the far right column in Figure 4.3, you'll see a 'PO No.' column. This refers to a purchase order created in QuickBooks, as shown in Figure 4.4.

Once a purchase order has been created, this is the only time substantial data entry is required by the book-keeper or some other person in the organisation. When goods are received, only the quantity of each item need be entered; when the invoice is received from the supplier, it is cross-referenced to the purchase order and, typically, all that is required is to check that the prices agree. As this process occurs, the stock of each item is updated and all relevant ledger accounts too. Can you imagine trying to do all this manually? It would be quite a lot of work. In Chapter 7 you'll learn more on keeping track of stocks in a business.

brilliant tip

Remember, if you buy accounting software, to be aware of the requirements of your business. For example, do you need to track stock as described above? It is always much easier to set up the software to do all you need it to do from day one.

Recording cash purchases

Most businesses purchase goods and services on credit. Cash purchases are always possible too, although this tends to happen more in small businesses that receive cash on a regular basis. Even when cash purchases do occur, the amounts are normally small and possibly from one-off suppliers.

Cash purchases can be recorded in two day books depending on the type of purchase. When cash is paid for one-off items and the amount is reasonably large, the transaction is normally recorded in the cash book. Cash purchases can be paid for in notes and coins, by cheque, credit card or any other immediate payment form. Chapter 5 will explain this type of cash purchase. When small amounts of cash are paid for purchases of goods or services on a more regular basis, the petty cash book is often used.

Many businesses have a petty cash box which is used to pay for small cash expenses or purchases. For example, tea or milk might be needed for the office kitchen, or the boss needs £2 to pay for parking. For such small expenditure it does not make a lot of sense to write a cheque or use a credit card, so the money is taken from the petty cash box.

Figure 4.5 shows an example of how a petty cash book might look.

Great Garages

Petty cash book

Date			Paid out Date		Vch. Ref.	Total	Teas	Cleaner	Office supplies
01/10/09	Balance	100.00	03/10/09	Tea	234	1.39	1.39		
31/10/09	Cheque	10.09	06/10/09	Window cleaner	235	5.50		5.50	
			07/10/09	Pens	236	3.20			3.20
				Total spend		10.09	1.39	5.50	3.20
			31/10/09	Balance		100.00			
		110.09				110.09			

Figure 4.5 Sample petty cash book

The layout of the petty cash book is similar to the day books we have already seen. This time, however, there are two 'sides' to the book. A petty cash book normally uses what is called an *imprest* system. This simply means that a certain petty cash balance is maintained and topped up. In Figure 4.5, the first entry on the left side shows that on 1 October, the opening balance of petty cash is £100. This should represent notes and coins held in a cash box or drawer by the book-keeper. The right-hand columns show the petty cash expenses, analysed by expense type. Each expense item is usually recorded on a petty cash voucher (you can buy these at any office supplies store) and a supporting receipt is attached to the voucher. The expenses are then totalled – £10.09 in the example. At the end of each month, a cheque for the amount of total expenses (i.e. £10.09) is cashed to replenish the balance to £100. You might be thinking this is a lot of effort for such a small amount of money. I agree! However, there may be instances where not keeping some form of petty cash system could create problems for you. Here are two examples.

First, any cash payments to employees could be deemed as income and thus taxable (see Chapter 6 for more on pay). Some years ago, I had to create a petty cash book for a small haulage business. In this case, drivers were often on longer trips and needed money for meals or overnight accommodation. The amounts were small and did not warrant drivers having credit cards, so they were given cash. Following a tax inspection, the business had to use a petty cash system for the drivers' expenses as the tax inspectors were not happy with cash being paid to employees without any supporting records.

The second example, while involving a small amount of petty cash, is a great example of the need to keep good records. In this case, the business made quarterly refund claims from a foreign VAT authority. The average refund amount was £100,000 per quarter. Each time the claim was sent, the postage (approximately £2) was recorded in the petty cash book, but without a receipt attached. One claim to the VAT authority went missing and this was not discovered for more than 12 months. The VAT authority had a 12-month time limit on claims. The business pleaded with the authority and they agreed that the claim could be resubmitted on proof of postage of the original claim. I'm sure you can guess what happened next. Yes, as no proof of postage/receipt was attached to the petty cash voucher the company could not resubmit the claim and thus lost the money, all £100,000. This example is a great reflection of what good book-keeping, even on the small things, can prevent.

Discounts and returns

Discounts

In the same way your business might give customers a discount, suppliers often will also offer discounts. This is called *discount received* and should be recorded separately. For example, many suppliers will give a discount for early payment. Normally, discounts are not recorded in the purchases day book but in the cash book, which you'll learn about in Chapter 5.

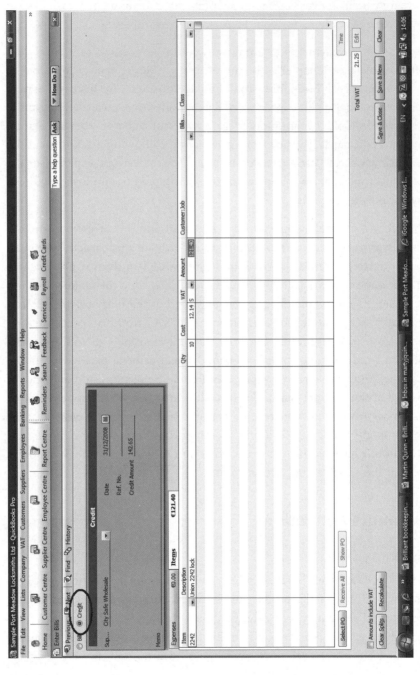

Figure 4.6 Entering a credit note in QuickBooks

Returns

If goods bought are faulty, incorrect or poor quality, it is normal to return them to the supplier. The supplier then issues a credit note, which reduces the amount owed to them. Returns are recorded in a *purchases returns day book*, which would have a layout just like the purchases day book shown in Figure 4.1. The purpose of recording returns separately is to use the information to query suppliers on issues such as quality, incorrect deliveries, etc. If the volume of returns to suppliers is low it might not be worthwhile keeping a purchases returns day book at all. In QuickBooks, the return of an item is entered in a similar way to a bill, except the option for credit is selected (see Figure 4.6).

Keeping track of returns of purchased goods is quite common where businesses follow strict quality control schemes. Again, consider the business needs before deciding whether or not you need a greater level of detail on returns. If you're using software like QuickBooks, as you can see, it is not too difficult.

Monitoring trade payables

We have seen in Chapter 3 that keeping track of what customers owe is important. Likewise, keeping an eye on what you owe suppliers is also important – although you might want to direct your attention to getting cash from customers first.

Once you record all credit purchases and expenses in a purchases day book or in some software it is possible to determine how much you owe each supplier – remember that every purchase gets posted to an individual supplier account. Of course, to get an up-to-date balance of what is owed to a supplier, you'll also need to record payments (see Chapter 5), discounts and returns. As with monitoring trade receivables, using software really helps the book-keeper to monitor trade payables. An aged payables report is usually a standard feature of accounting software. Figure 4.7 shows an aged payables report in QuickBooks.

In this example, you can see the amounts owed to suppliers according to the age of the debt. Each supplier might offer different credit terms, so this report can be a little misleading. However, it does allow a book-keeper easily to assess how long suppliers are owed money and subsequently pay

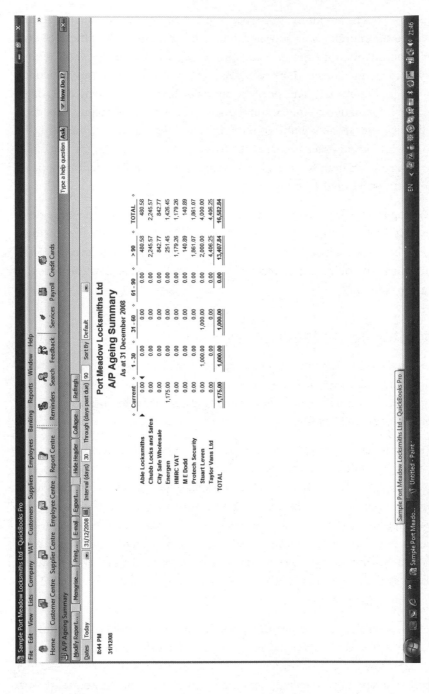

Figure 4.7 Aged payables report in QuickBooks

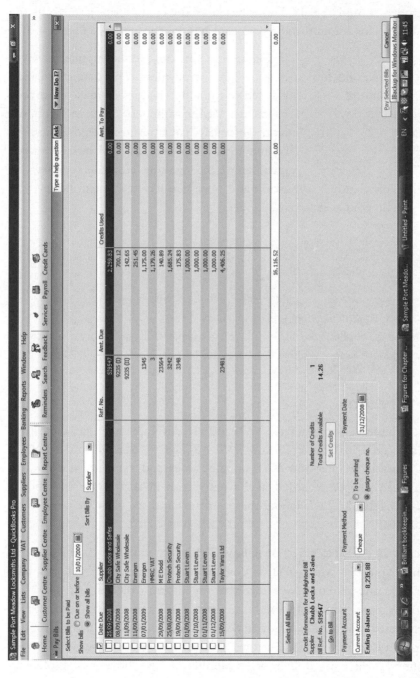

Figure 4.8 Selecting supplier invoices for payment in QuickBooks

them. In fact, most accounting software will automatically suggest which suppliers should be paid. This is based on the credit terms granted by the supplier. The amounts to be paid can then be chosen – see Figure 4.8.

once you have collected money, you should do your best to pay suppliers

In Figure 4.8, you can see the supplier invoices that are due for payment. This listing can then be used to draw up cheques or make electronic payments. Paying suppliers on time is impor- tant. Obviously, your business requires cash to be able to pay suppliers, so most businesses put great effort into getting customers to pay on time. This clearly is a must do and once you have collected money, you should do your best to pay suppliers.

brilliant tip

Try to adopt a regular and systematic approach to paying suppliers. Always pay your most important suppliers first and then work down the list. This ensures your business will be less likely to experience suppliers not delivering important materials/services you need due to monies owing.

VAT returns

Most businesses register for VAT and effectively become tax collectors. You've seen in Chapter 3 how VAT on sales is charged and recorded and in this chapter how VAT on purchases and expenses is recorded. VAT can also be recorded in the petty cash book and the cash books (see Chapter 5). Let's ignore these for now and see what we need to do with VAT.

Here's an example based on UK VAT, but the core idea is the same in other countries where VAT is charged. In the UK, the VAT amounts on sales and purchases are recorded on a form called a VAT 100. The form is more commonly referred to as a 'VAT return'. This form can be completed manually, but nowadays is more likely to be filled out online through HM Revenue & Customs' website (www.hmrc.gov.uk). Whether online or paper-based, there are a number of input boxes to complete on the form. Only the more common input boxes are dealt with here.

The figures that go into the boxes described here are the totals of the VAT amounts for a time period. This might be two, three or even six months. The totals are obtained from the day books. Again, accounting software is quite helpful and often can produce a VAT 100 report in a mouse click.

Box 1

This box contains the total VAT charged on sales. This usually is termed 'VAT on outputs'. In a manual set of books, the figure would be the total of all VAT columns from the sales day book, the sales returns day book (a deduction) and the cash book – if cash sales are present. The figures might also come from your accounting software or perhaps from a cash register printout.

Box 4

In this box, you enter the total amount of VAT paid on purchases and expenses. Such VAT is usually termed 'VAT on inputs'. This figure would be the total of all VAT columns from the purchases day book – net of purchases returns – and any VAT in the cheque payments or cash books. Again, this figure can come from your accounting software.

Box 5

This box contains the VAT owing to HM Revenue & Customs or the amount due to be repaid to you. It is simply the difference between the output VAT (Box 1) and the input VAT (Box 4). Amounts owed usually are due to the tax authorities within two to three weeks of the period to which the VAT return relates. Late payment can incur interest charges.

Figure 4.9 shows a report produced by QuickBooks which can be used to complete the VAT 100. Such a report is almost guaranteed to be a feature of any accounting software and is customised for the country or locality.

brilliant tip

Treat monies owed for VAT as very important. You should never delay payment as it can lead to an inspection of your business records by the tax authorities. Making sure all business transactions are recorded in a timely fashion helps get the VAT return done on time.

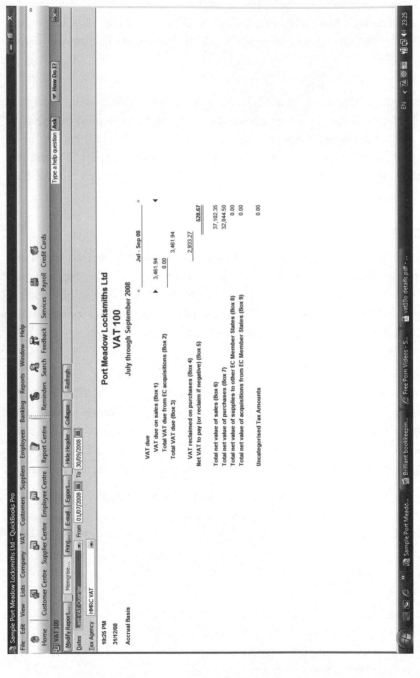

Figure 4.9 VAT 100 report in QuickBooks

Completing the VAT 100 form is the easy part of course. VAT can be a complex area and you should seek advice from an accountant if you are in any doubt about what VAT rate to charge or whether you can claim VAT on all inputs. The most important role for the book-keeper is to ensure data needed for VAT returns is captured in an accurate and timely fashion.

> ensure data needed is captured in an accurate and timely fashion

 brilliant recap

- Purchases and expenses on credit are recorded in a purchases day book.

- Accounting software offers substantial advantages over manual records in the recording of purchases and expenses.

- Small cash purchases are often recorded in a petty cash book using an imprest system.

- Returns to suppliers can be recorded in a purchases returns day book if required. Normally, a supplier will issue a credit note to the value of returned goods.

- Monitoring trade payables is important. The use of an aged payables report from your accounting software is helpful.

- VAT recorded on sales (outputs) and purchases/expenses (inputs) is used to complete a VAT return.

CHAPTER 5

Recording and monitoring cash

I n this chapter you'll learn the book-keeping issues (and understand control issues) around cash receipts and payments. The previous two chapters dealt with recording sales and purchases. Cash is received from sales and is paid for purchases of goods and expenses. For book-keeping purposes, it doesn't matter when the cash is paid, or its form, e.g. cheque, direct debit. All cash, with the exception of petty cash (see Chapter 4), is recorded in some form of cash book.

> all cash, with the exception of petty cash, is recorded in some form of cash book

First we'll revisit the accruals concept that underpins accounting. You'll then learn how cash is recorded in a manual book-keeping system. Typically, two day books are used, the *cash receipts book* and the *cheque payments book*. You'll then see how cash transactions are handled in QuickBooks. Next, you'll learn a very simple but effective way to verify the book-keeping work you have done so far. This process, called bank reconciliation, is very important and needs to be done on a regular basis. Finally, you'll learn some additional controls that a book-keeper might impose in a business where a high volume of cash is present.

Accruals accounting

Accruals accounting basically says that profit is the difference between revenue and expenses, not between cash received and paid (see also Chapter 2). As shown in Chapters 3 and 4, goods and services are bought and sold on credit and paid for at a later date. Therefore, what we use as income (or sales revenue) and expenses when calculating our profits may or may not correspond with the cash received or paid. In Chapter 9 you'll learn more about calculating profits.

You might be thinking now, hang on, if cash is not the basis for calculating profits, why do I need to bother recording cash in my books? The answer is two-fold. First, recording cash received from credit customers and paid to credit suppliers allows you to determine the amounts of money owed by customers or to suppliers. In other words, recording cash allows the book-keeper to keep track of these important assets and liabilities of a business. Second, not all businesses offer credit, nor are all sales and expenses on credit, so cash sales and expenses must be captured.

Now let's see how we record cash receipts and payments, starting with an example of how a manual cash book might look, and then how QuickBooks handles cash.

Recording cash receipts

Cash receipts mainly come from the sale of products or services. If a business grants credit, then the sale has already been recorded and the payment is received later. Other sources of cash might be the sale of assets, e.g. a business sells some old equipment. As shown in previous chapters for sales and purchases, the detail in which you record cash in your books depends on the level of detail you need. The simplest classification might be cash from sales/customers and 'other' cash.

Before showing you how cash receipts are recorded in a manual book-keeping system, it is important to clarify what we mean by cash. Nowadays, very few businesses deal purely in hard cash, i.e. notes and coins. Receipts and payments are usually in the form of cheques or even direct transfers in and out of bank accounts. If your business is mainly cash, like a pub or fast-food outlet, you are likely to bank any cash regularly and make payments by cheque or electronic transfer. There are, however, still some businesses where cash is used to pay suppliers before being banked. For example, a fast-food outlet might pay a potato grower in cash each week for potatoes used to make chips. Paying out cash in this way makes no difference to cash receipts as they should be recorded in full before payments are made. In such a business, then, what I call a 'full cash book' might be required. A sample of this type of cash book is shown later, but let's first look at a typical cash receipts book.

Figure 5.1 shows an example of a typical cash receipts book for a business that has mainly credit sales.

Great Garages

Cash receipts book

Date		Ref.	Total	Debtors	Sales 15%	Sales 25%	Other	VAT	Lodged
01/10/2009	Cash sales		115		100			15	
02/10/2009	John Adams	456	2,000	2,000					2,115
06/10/2009	Cash sales	457	125			100		25	125
25/10/2009	James O'Toole	458	3,750	3,750					3,750
31/10/2009	Mary Carpenter		500	500					
31/10/2009	Refund of water charges	459	10				10		510
			6,500	6,250	100	100	10	40	6,500

Figure 5.1 Sample cash receipts book

This cash receipts book shows columns for cash received from trade debtors (customers), cash sales at varying VAT rates, other cash receipts and a VAT column. A 'total' column shows the total of the cash received for each line, while a 'lodged' column shows the amount of money lodged in the business bank account. The 'ref.' column is used in this example to enter a lodgement reference, which is usually a pre-printed number on a lodgement book provided by the bank.

The cash receipts from debtors are paying amounts they owe the business. VAT is irrelevant for these payments as the VAT has already been captured in the sales day book. Thus, while the cash received on 2 October from John Adams in Figure 5.1 includes VAT, the VAT element is not recorded again. However, when a cash sale is made (as on 1 October and 6 October in Figure 5.1), any VAT has not been captured previously so it should be recorded. The 'other' column captures cash received from one-off or unusual sources, such as a refund of water charges in Figure 5.1. Any cash receipts recorded in an 'other' column usually are not related to the sale of goods and services.

The source documents for the cash receipts book normally will be records of amounts lodged in the business bank account. Normally the book-keeper will add together cheques and cash for a day (or other time period) and then make a single bank lodgement. Figure 5.1, for example, shows a lodgement with the reference 456 for £2,115, which is the sum of two receipts. In small businesses, the make-up of lodgements often is written on a piece of paper or on the back of the stub in the lodgement book provided by the bank. We'll see in QuickBooks later that this process is made simple when many cash receipts are combined to make a lodgement.

brilliant tip

It is a good idea to take photocopies of the cheques you receive from customers. It's a great help having copies when cheques get lost or stolen. If the volume of cheques is large, you could consider scanning them electronically or, better still, reduce the number of cheques by asking customers to pay directly into your bank account. If you do want to get paid electronically, why not put bank details on your sales invoice?

Once cash has been recorded in the cash receipts book, it is also entered in a number of other places. As with the day books already described in previous chapters, the totals of each column are used to update the nominal ledger. Looking at Figure 5.1, for example, the amount owed by customers in the debtors account will decrease by £6,250, cash sales will increase by £200 (£100 + £100), water charges will reduce by £10, and the VAT owed will increase by £40. And, of course, the bank account will increase by the total cash lodged, i.e. £6,500. For each cash receipt in the 'debtors' column, the amount of cash is recorded on each customer account in the personal ledger too. For example, the amount John Adams owes is reduced by £2,000. Again, Chapter 8 will provide more detail on ledger accounts.

Now let's see how to record cash payments that might be made from cash before being lodged. Figure 5.2 shows an example.

The example in Figure 5.2 is of a traditional type fast-food outlet, i.e. the good old chippy. I have done book-keeping in the past for a number of such outlets. As you can guess, such a business receives mainly hard cash. They also typically pay smaller suppliers and wages in cash before banking the remainder. There is nothing wrong in making such cash payments, once they are recorded and supported with documentation. In Figure 5.2, you can see the daily takings figure on the left-hand side. These figures would come from a reconciliation of the cash in the cash register(s) each day (see later in this chapter). On the right-hand side, you

Fryer Tuck's Fast Food

Cash Book

Date		Receipts	Date		Total	Wages	Purchases
01/08/2009	Daily takings	510	03/08/2009	Wages	240	240	
02/08/2009	Daily takings	348	05/08/2009	Potatoes	40		40
03/08/2009	Daily takings	230	06/08/2009	Milk	16		16
04/08/2009	Daily takings	245	06/08/2009	Redland Fishmongers	67		67
05/08/2009	Daily takings	450					
06/08/2009	Daily takings	890					
07/08/2009	Daily takings	658					
	Total takings for week	3,331	Total cash paid		363	240	123
			Lodged to bank		2,968		
		3,331			3,331		

Figure 5.2 Sample cash book for a cash business

can see items that were paid for in cash and these are analysed as either wages or purchases. There could of course be more columns. The cash balance left over, £2,968, is then lodged to the bank. As with the other day books we have seen, the totals are used to update the nominal ledger accounts. In this case, though, each line is not used to update the personal accounts of suppliers as the payments are made in cash, so no amounts are ever owed and we don't need to keep track of them.

As with all other day books you've seen, the exact layout will be determined by the business requirements, but the examples given are a good starting point.

Cash receipts in QuickBooks

Now let's see how cash receipts are recorded in QuickBooks. As in a manual book-keeping system, how cash is recorded depends on the source. If cash is received from a credit customer (debtor), then we need to not only record the cash but also update the customer's account with the payment. If the receipt is from cash sales or some other source, it is recorded in a slightly different way. You've already seen in Chapter 3 (see Figure 3.4, p. 39) how QuickBooks deals with receipts from cash sales, so let's see first how cash receipts from debtors are processed and then how other types of cash receipts are recorded. In all cases, it is assumed that any cash is lodged to a business bank account.

Figure 5.3 shows how QuickBooks records a cash receipt from a debtor.

In this example, a customer called Hertford Surgery is making a payment of £1,365.67 for two invoices as shown. You can also see that this amount

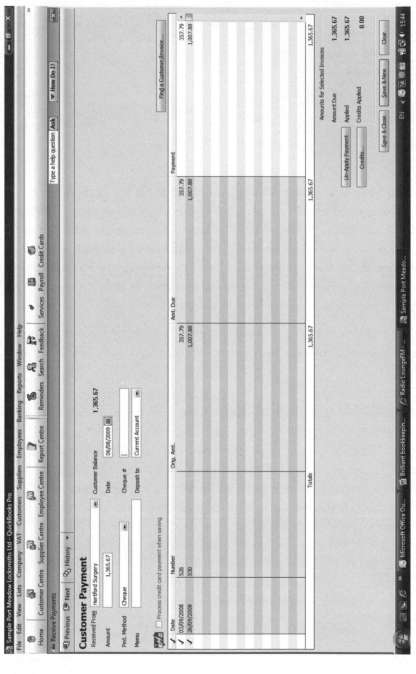

Figure 5.3   Recording cash received from debtors in QuickBooks

of cash is to be deposited to the 'Current Account', meaning it is lodged directly to the bank. There is quite a lot going on here in book-keeping terms:

● The cash receipt is being recorded.

● The bank balance (in the nominal ledger) is updated by the amount of cash received.

● The customer's account is updated to show that two invoices have been paid and they now owe less.

● The nominal ledger is also updated to reflect that the total amount owing from all customers is now less.

Here again, it is easy to appreciate the advantages of using software, as multiple tasks are completed while entering a single transaction.

> it is easy to appreciate the advantages of using software

In Figure 5.3, the amount of cash received is taken as being lodged directly to a bank account as a single receipt. This is not normally the case. More often, a business will group cheques received from customers and make one lodgement from several receipts. QuickBooks also caters for this by using a temporary account called 'Undeposited Funds'.

Figures 5.4 to 5.6 show how multiple cash receipts can be grouped as one lodgement in QuickBooks. Figures 5.4 and 5.5 show two separate cash receipts from two different customers. You can see how, in both cases, the cash receipt is recorded as being deposited to 'Undeposited Funds'. When you have finished entering cash receipts, you can then select them as shown in Figure 5.6 to make a single lodgement (or 'Deposit' in QuickBooks terminology) to the bank account. The highlighted area shows where the money is being lodged (the 'Current Account') and the total you can see is the sum of the two receipts from Figures 5.4 and 5.5. This method of entering cash receipts most likely is the method you'll use in QuickBooks or other accounting software. Lodging cash can of course be avoided by getting customers to pay direct to your bank account, but achieving this for all your customers is not an easy job.

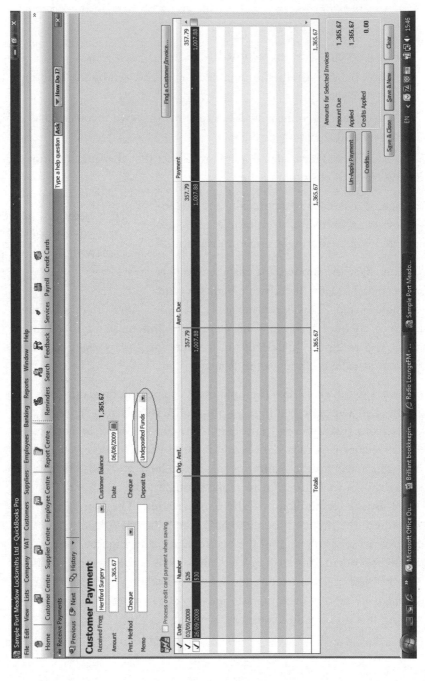

Figure 5.4 Cash receipt from Hertford Surgery

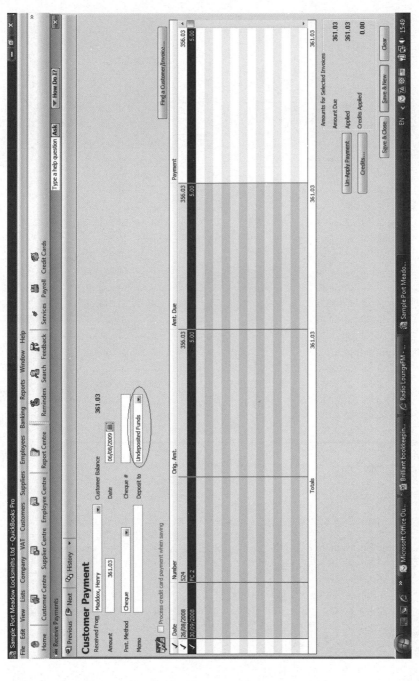

Figure 5.5 Cash receipt from Henry Maddox

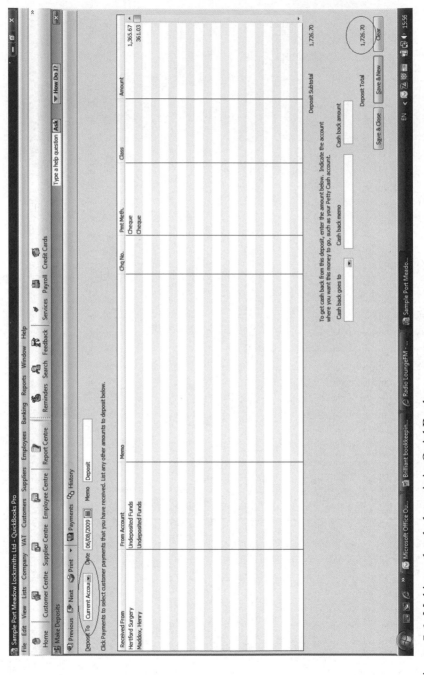

Figure 5.6 Making a bank deposit in QuickBooks

brilliant tip

When matching cash receipts against customer invoices, always try to match cash receipts against the oldest invoices owed. Even better, encourage customers to pay the oldest invoices first and discourage them from paying even amounts 'on account'. This is not always possible, but does help to keep your records tidy.

Recording cash payments

You have learned how cash payments can be recorded in a cash book before being lodged (see Figure 5.2 p. 73). More often, businesses use non-cash forms of payment, such as cheques, direct debits, standing orders and bank transfers. Cheques need no explanation and are still a common form of payment. If your business uses a cheque book, be sure that the stubs are always fully completed (with date, amount and payee) as they are valuable source documents. Direct debits and standing orders are similar in that they are electronic payment methods. They are often used to pay business loans, utility bills, rent, etc. A direct debit can vary in amount, whereas a standing order is a fixed amount. Bank transfers (using the SWIFT system) are quite common in larger businesses and are increasingly commonplace in smaller businesses. Paying suppliers or staff using bank transfer will mean you need to provide your bank with a file for processing. Most accounting and payroll software can do this, but do check before you buy as banks have very specific requirements.

In a manual book-keeping system, excluding payments made in notes and coins, all other forms of payment are usually captured in the cheque payments book. The source documents for the cheque payments book are the stubs of the business cheque book and bank statements, the latter being used to pick up direct debits, standing orders and bank transfers. You might also have a record of the amounts of each standing order, debit or transfer elsewhere, but the bank statement is an easy place to find them all.

 **brilliant** tip

Ensure your bank sends you a statement at least once a month. Better still, why not get online access to the business bank account? Regular checking of the bank statements ensures you capture electronic payments and receipts as soon as possible.

How you decide to lay out a cheque payments book depends as always on the level of detail to be captured. Normally, a cheque payments book will have a column for amounts paid to suppliers (creditors) and several other columns for expenses and other payments. Figure 5.7 shows an example of a cheque payments book.

Great Garages

Cheque payments

Date		Chq. Ref.	Total	Creditors	Light and heat	Wages	Phone	VAT	Misc.
03/10/2009	AB Supplies Ltd	500789	3,400	3,400					
06/10/2009	Electricity company	500790	130		130				
07/10/2009	Staff wages	500791	500			500			
08/10/2009	Telephone company	DD	120				120		
18/10/2009	Hill Motors – new van	DD	15,000						15,000
23/10/2009	Taxation authorities	DD	3,000					3,000	
31/10/2009	Petty cash	500792	10						10
31/10/2009	Factor Ltd	500793	4,570	4,570					
			26,730	7,970	130	500	120	3,000	15,010

Figure 5.7 Sample cheque payments book

In this example, a relatively simple cheque payments book is shown. It has a total column, six analysis columns and the normal date, reference and narrative columns. The 'creditors' column shows amounts paid to suppliers from whom goods/services were bought on credit. These amounts would have been recorded previously as a purchase in the purchases day book. All other columns to the right of the 'creditors' column are effectively recording payments for expenses, liabilities or assets, which did not go through the purchases day book, or, in other words, where credit has not been given. Note that the amount shown in the VAT column in Figure 5.7 is the amount paid over to the tax authorities, which is from the VAT 100 form (see Chapter 4, p. 64). It is also possible that you might capture VAT on a one-off payment here, so be careful what you put in the VAT column. You might prefer to put VAT paid to the tax authorities in an 'other' or 'miscellaneous' column.

As mentioned, the layout of a cheque payments book will depend on what the requirements are but, as you can imagine, if you have, say, 20 columns in your book, it becomes a little cluttered. As book-keeper, you can decide to put most bills from suppliers through the purchases day book if you wish. This means that the vast majority of cheques will appear as creditor payments, and appear under the 'creditors' column as in Figure 5.7.

brilliant tip

If you deal with a supplier on a regular basis, even twice or three times a year, you can record invoices/bills received in the purchases day book, even if a payment was made immediately. This keeps the cheque payments book tidy in a manual book-keeping system and also allows you to see if you have forgotten to pay someone.

As with all other day books, the totals from the cheque payments book are used as a source to update nominal ledger accounts. The sum of the 'total' column reduces the bank balance. The total of the 'creditors' column reduces the total amount owed to suppliers, while each payment from this column reduces the amount owed to each individual supplier and is reflected in the personal ledger. The totals of other columns will increase an expense (e.g. light and heat, wages and phone in Figure 5.7), decrease a liability (e.g. the VAT paid in Figure 5.7), or increase an asset (the purchase of the new van in Figure 5.7). It is quite normal to have a 'sundry' or 'miscellaneous' column in a cheque payments book. This is then further analysed by an accountant when preparing accounts. In the example in Figure 5.7, the total would be broken down into £15,000 for the new van and £10 to petty cash. These would in turn be posted to their respective nominal ledger accounts. We'll see more on ledger accounts in Chapter 8.

Now that you have an appreciation of how payments are recorded using a cheque payments book, let's see how QuickBooks deals with them.

Recording cash payments in QuickBooks

Accounting software usually distinguishes between payments to suppliers (i.e. creditors) and other payments for one-off items or expenses like

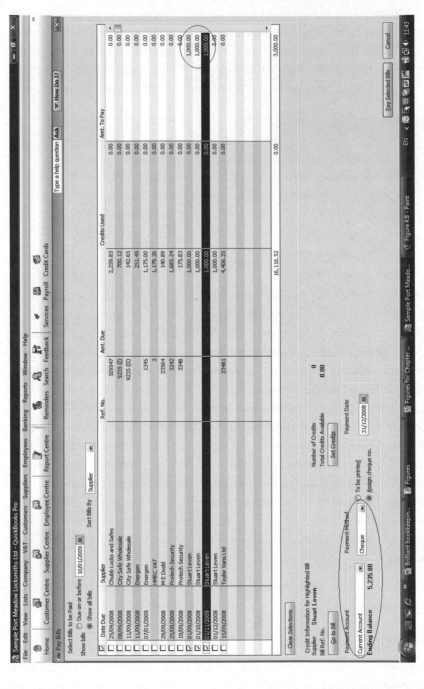

Figure 5.8 Selecting bills for payment in QuickBooks

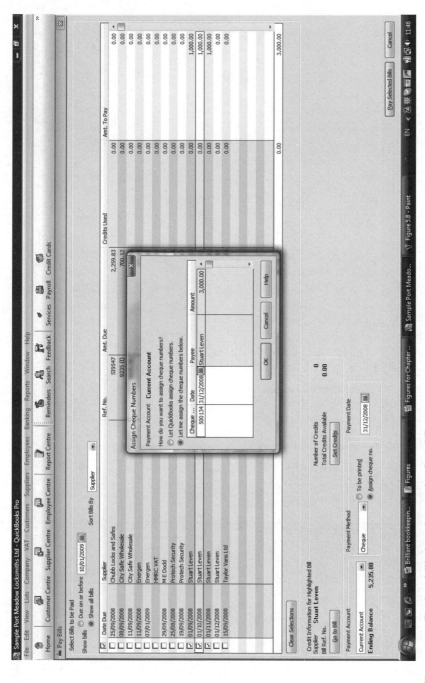

Figure 5.9 Paying bills by cheque in QuickBooks

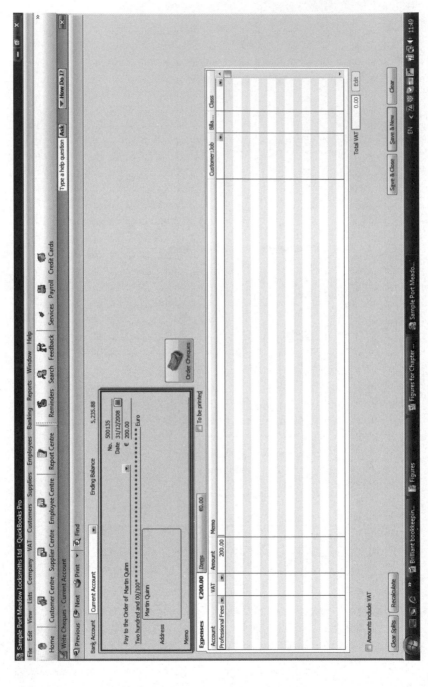

Figure 5.10 Recording a cheque payment in QuickBooks

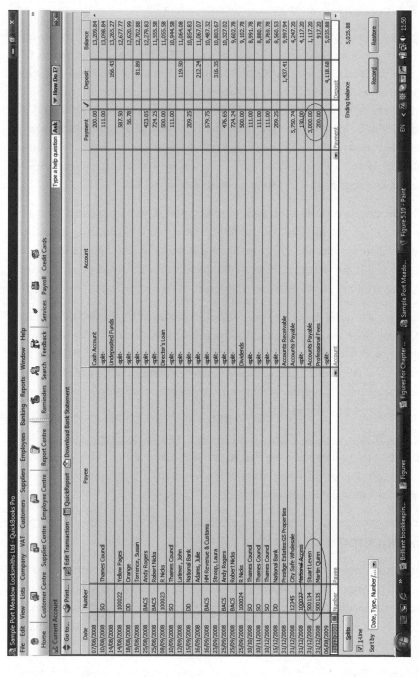

Figure 5.11 The bank account in QuickBooks

wages. You have already seen how QuickBooks pays suppliers (see Figure 4.8, p. 61), but let's now get a little more detail.

As noted in Chapter 4, QuickBooks uses the term 'bills' to describe supplier invoices and other invoices received for goods or services. In Figure 5.8 you can see that QuickBooks presents a list of invoices which it regards as due for payment. Three invoices from the supplier Stuart Leven are selected for payment. The payment totals £3,000 and the money will be paid by cheque from the business current account (see the encircled areas). Once all invoices for payment are selected, you simply click on 'Pay Selected Bills' and then enter a payment reference (the cheque number in this case), as shown in Figure 5.9.

This process is repeated for each supplier that is to be paid and is equivalent to filling out the cheque payments book and putting the amount in the 'creditors' column. Of course, in addition to this, QuickBooks will update the bank account, reduce the total amount owed to all suppliers and the amount owed by Stuart Leven.

Making payments for other, non-supplier items in QuickBooks is slightly different. Such payments would be similar to those shown in the cheque payments book in Figure 5.7, i.e. wages, utility bills, etc. Figure 5.10 shows how to record such a cheque payment in QuickBooks. Of course, it might not be a cheque, rather a direct debit or standing order, but the method would be the same.

Finally, if you look at Figure 5.11, which shows the bank account from QuickBooks, you can see the two payments made above. This again shows the key advantage of using software over manual records, which is that you need enter data only once.

Reconciling the bank

You know now that bank statements are a source document for the cheque payments book. Monies can come in and out of the business bank account unnoticed by the book-keeper. One of the most common examples is bank interest and charges, although most banks now notify interest and charges to customers in advance.

Normally banks send statements at least once a month to business customers, and most now provide secure online services, which means the balance and history of the bank account are always accessible. Now let's think for a moment about the day books we have seen in this chapter, namely the cash receipts book and the cheque payments book. If we know the balance in the bank account at the start of a month, add the total of the cash receipts book to this balance and deduct the total of the cheque payments book, then we should have a balance that is the same as the balance on the bank statement at the end of the month. Do you agree?

Try to jot down reasons why you think there might be differences between the two.

There are a number of reasons why the balance between your records and the banks might be different.

1   As already mentioned, there could be receipts or payments in/out of the bank that you have not recorded in your books.

2   You could have made a mistake in your books. For example, the totals are added up wrong, a problem that is easily avoided using spreadsheets or accounting software. Or, a mistake has been made in one of the books, for example £500 was written as £50.

3   There may be timing differences. For example, you may have written a cheque to a supplier and recorded it correctly in the cheque payments book or in your accounting software, but the supplier has not yet cashed it, so the money is still in your bank account.

Finding differences such as these is called 'bank reconciliation'. As an accountant, I really love it when I see a set of books where the bank has been reconciled. What it means is that first, the difference between the bank balances has been explained and second, every other transaction in the books has been verified as correct with the bank statement. For example, if a sale has been made and the cash received and lodged in the bank, we know the transaction is correct. Likewise, when a payment is made to a supplier or for wages, etc. we can be sure the figures are correct by checking them against the bank statement. So, if you want to keep your books in the best possible shape and keep your accountant happy, be sure to do a bank reconciliation on a regular basis. Small businesses might do one monthly, with larger businesses doing one more regularly. Now, let's see how it's done using the sample cash receipts book and cheques payments book from Figures 5.1 and 5.7. Look back at these when you need to.

Take a look at Figure 5.12, which shows a bank statement of the sample business used earlier, Great Garages. Let's assume the balance at 1 October has already been reconciled with the books of the business.

First Bank plc

Statement as at 31/10/2009

Account of: *Great Garages*

		Ref.	Debit	Credit	Balance
1 Oct.	Opening balance				5,437
3 Oct.	Lodgement	456		2115	7,552
3 Oct.	Cheque	500789	3,400		4,152
6 Oct.	Lodgement	457		125	4,277
	Cheque	500790	130		4,147
8 Oct.	Cheque	500791	500		3,647
	Debit	DD	210		3,437
18 Oct.	Debit	DD	15,000		–11,563
19 Oct.	Interest & charges	DD	15		–11,578
24 Oct.	Debit	DD	3,000		–14,578
25 Oct.	Lodgement	458		3,750	–10,828

Figure 5.12 Bank statement of Great Garages

Looking at the statement, you can see a 'credit' column which shows monies lodged in the bank, and a 'debit' column showing monies paid out. If everything in our books is in tandem with the bank, the closing balance we calculate should be the same as shown on the statement, i.e. £10,828, which means it is overdrawn. Let's do a quick sum. The totals of the cash receipts and cheque payments are taken from Figures 5.1 and 5.7.

Closing bank balance of Great Garages

Balance as at 1 Oct.	£5,437
Add cash received and lodged	£6,500
Less cheques	(£26,730)
Balance as at 31 Oct.	(£14, 793)

The balance above is negative or overdrawn. The balance per the bank statements is £10,828 overdrawn, so we need to reconcile (or explain) why this difference occurs. In the process, we might find some errors in our books. You don't need to do this sum when doing the reconciliation, it just helps explain things here.

brilliant tip

When doing a bank reconciliation, it is normal to take the figures on the bank statements as being correct rather than your own figures. Banks have been around for quite a while and have tried and tested systems. Having said that, they do make mistakes so keep an eye open if any difference is substantial.

To find the difference, we need to compare each item on the bank statement with our books. I like to start with the lodgements, so look at each item in the lodged column in Figure 5.1 versus the credit column on the bank statement. When you do this in real life, it's a good idea to tick each item with a pen. You would tick each item in the lodged column of the cash receipts book and on the bank statement once the amounts matched. In this example you'll find that lodgement number 459, for £510, is not on the bank statement. This is one part of the difference.

Now compare each item on the cheque payments book with the bank statement. The first difference you should spot is the amount paid for telephone by direct debit on 8 October. It has been recorded as £120 in the cheque payments book, but in fact went through the bank for £210. Let's assume the bank was right, and correct the amount in the cheque payments book. The next item that is different is the bank interest and charges of £15 on 19 October, which is not in the books so it should be recorded. Finally, cheque numbers 500792 and 500793, for £10 and £4,570 respectively, are not on the bank statement. This means they have not yet been cashed and are thus outstanding. Again you should tick each item with a pen as they agree. Doing this, you can easily spot items like the two outstanding cheques, as they won't be ticked.

As we have spotted two differences in the cheque payments book, Figure 5.13 shows a corrected version.

Great Garages

Cheque payments

Date		Chq. Ref.	Total	Creditors	Light and heat	Wages	Phone	VAT	Misc.
03/10/2009	AB Supplies Ltd	500789	3,400	3,400					
06/10/2009	Electricity company	500790	130		130				
07/10/2009	Staff wages	500791	500			500			
08/10/2009	Telephone company	DD	210				210		
18/10/2009	Hill Motors – new van	DD	15,000						15,000
19/10/2009	Bank interest/charges	DD	15						15
23/10/2009	Taxation authorities	DD	3,000					3,000	
31/10/2009	Petty cash	500792	10						10
31/10/2009	Factor Ltd	500793	4,570	4,570					
			26,835	7,970	130	500	210	3,000	15,025

Figure 5.13 Cheque payments book of Great Garages after comparison with the bank statement

Now, we can do our sum again.

Closing bank balance of Great Garages

Balance as at 1 Oct.	£5,437
Add cash received and lodged	£6,500
Less cheques	(£26,835)
Balance as at 31 Oct.	(£14,898)

We can now explain the difference between what our records say we should have in the bank and what the bank statement says. Figure 5.14 shows how. This simple sum usually is called a *bank reconciliation statement*.

First, the balance per the bank statement is shown. From this, any outstanding cheques are deducted. This is because our records have already recorded these as paid from the bank, but they have not yet been cashed. Then, any outstanding lodgements are added, as these are in our books but have not yet cleared the bank. Doing this sum, you can see that the figure is now (£14,898), which is the same as calculated earlier. Thus, now we have explained why there is a difference between what the bank says we have and what our records say. The amount of money in the bank has not changed in any way, but we now know why the difference exists. Timing differences that cause cheques or lodgements to be outstanding

Great Garages

Bank reconciliation as at 31 Oct.

		£
Balance per bank statement		(10,828)
Less outstanding cheques		
	500792	(10)
	500793	(4,570)
		(15,408)
Add outstanding lodgements		
	459	510
Balance per our records		(14,898)

Figure 5.14 Bank reconciliation for Great Garages

are common, but are diminishing as more bank transactions are made electronically.

In QuickBooks, the bank reconciliation process is quite similar, except that you are presented with a list of cheque payments and cash receipts on-screen. You select any amounts that agree with the bank statement and QuickBooks then does the bank reconciliation automatically for you. For businesses with large volumes of transactions on the bank account, some accounting software can download a statement from the bank. It then attempts to do the reconciliation automatically, leaving the book-keeper to resolve anything it cannot find.

For the book-keeper and/or business owner, the bank balance is a very important figure. Having enough cash to pay debts as they fall due is the life-blood of a business. Therefore, it's a really good idea to keep your records in line with the bank statements at any time. Do a reconciliation at least once a month and check the bank account online more frequently so that you can record transactions like direct debits or credit transfers on the account.

> having enough cash to pay debts as they fall due is the life-blood of a business

Other controls on cash

Having looked at how cash is recorded in the books of a business, now let's turn our attention to some other tasks you might be faced with as a book-keeper. These tasks relate more to businesses that have a larger volume of cash-based transactions, i.e. notes and coins.

Despite the increased use of debit and credit cards, most retail businesses still handle cash. If you are a book-keeper in such a business, there are a number of controls you need to know about. Some of these might require the owner or manager to be involved too, but as book-keeper it is useful to be aware of how best to manage controls on cash.

The controls on cash can be classified as traditional 'low-tech' and other more 'high-tech' approaches. The former are common in most businesses to some degree, while the latter tend to be reserved for larger businesses with higher volumes of cash.

Traditional cash controls

The tried and trusted controls around cash aim to ensure that cash received in the business stays in the business. You've probably had the experience of walking into a shop early in the morning with a £50 note in your pocket to be told by the person at the cash register that they cannot take it as they have no change for you. The reason for having no change is that most retailers limit the amount of cash in their registers at any time. First thing in the morning, cash is likely to be at a minimum as few sales have taken place. In large retail outlets like supermarkets, you'll often see the cash register staff placing cash in a small plastic chute which takes it to a centralised and secure cash room. And I'm sure you have heard news reports of criminals having been caught when a dye-packed cash container exploded on them. As cash is the ultimate untraceable form of money, it thus deserves adequate controls.

The most obvious control has just been described above, i.e. restricting access to cash. Depending on the business these controls might include:

- keeping cash in a locked safe overnight
- regularly emptying cash registers and taking cash to a safe or secure cash room
- keeping larger bank notes out of hand's reach

- securing cash in transit – usually by using an external contractor to transport cash to banks

- varying routines – many smaller business owners often bring cash home at night. It's not something I would do, but if you do, vary the route you take home to prevent criminals establishing a profile on you/your business. This also might be good advice if you as book-keeper bring cash to the bank to be lodged.

These controls are aimed primarily at preventing cash being stolen by thieves. You will also need internal controls to limit the possibilities for employees to pocket cash. You might, like me, assume people are reasonably honest but, nonetheless, failure to control staff who can access cash might reduce your profits. In a cash business, cash register staff are responsible for recording every sale. They are thus a vital source of data for your recording of sales. The basic controls you should have in place are as follows:

- Assurance that every sale is recorded in the cash register. Supervision is one way to do this. Another option is to use barcode scanners at cash registers. Neither is foolproof, but both act as good deterrents.

- Unannounced spot checks. Modern point-of-sale (POS) cash registers can produce a printout of the total sales recorded by each staff member at any time during the day. This should equate to the amount of cash in the drawer, less any starting float of cash. If not, then questions need to be asked. If the amount of cash is considerably more than it should be, then it is likely that the employee has not recorded cash sales and may intend to pocket the cash. Older non-POS cash registers produce what often is called an 'X' or 'Z' read at the end of the day. Again, the totals per this report should equal the cash in the register drawer.

- A requirement for supervisor approval for changes to price or for refunds. Cash registers allow the pre-programming of prices for goods and POS-based systems contain full product and price data. If an employee can change a price, they can key in a lower value and pocket the difference. This is prevented by needing supervisor authorisation, which may be by means of a code entry. Likewise, cash refunds to customers should not be permitted without authorisation as an employee could record a dummy refund and pocket the cash.

- A requirement that staff explain differences in cash balances. Most retailers will ask staff to run a cash register summary at the end of the business day. If the total does not correspond to the amount of cash in the register drawer, then the staff member must explain why. Many retailers don't allow employees to finish work until all cash is accounted for, which usually is a good incentive to keep things right.

- Check employee history. It's always a good idea to phone previous employers and check references given by employees. While you may not be able to get specific information, you might be able to get a 'gut feeling' for the type of person the prospective employee is.

You may have noticed that a second person is involved in many of the controls mentioned. Separating duties is always a very useful way to control many aspects of business. The practicality of separating duties depends on the size of the business, but is always a good idea when possible. It may be possible to insure a business against losses from fraud or embezzlement, so as book-keeper you might want to check out any available options.

Using technology to control cash

The latest technology is often called upon to help control cash when some of the controls mentioned previously fail. For example, even if you segregate duties between a supervisor and employee, what is to stop them working as a team? The following controls might be used either when you strongly suspect staff are pocketing cash or when high volumes of cash are handled.

- Use barcode scanners (POS systems) at all cash registers. Coupled with the controls already described, this limits the possibility for staff to manipulate what is (or is not) entered into the register. In a POS cash register system, detailed reports by staff members can be run at any time. Watch the next time you're in Tesco or Sainsbury when a new staff member comes to a register – you'll see they key in an ID number or name, which attaches all cash received to them.

- Install hidden cameras that monitor the cash register. Many busy pubs have such systems. Cameras can even be linked to a remote location using the internet so business owners or other staff can monitor cash points. At the very least, any pocketed cash might be captured on camera, which can then be used as evidence.

● Mark notes. If you can pinpoint cash losses to a specific location, it is possible to 'arrange' a sale using secretly marked notes. For example, I know a milkman who had suspicions that his helper was pocketing some cash. He marked notes with an ultraviolet pen and left the marked notes on top of his 'cash box', which was a cardboard box in his living room. The notes were subsequently found in the helper's pocket. You'll often see retailers mark large notes with the objective that at least those notes won't be stolen.

Not all the controls on cash that are mentioned are applicable to all businesses. As book-keeper you often will be faced with implementing and following up on some of these controls. At a minimum, it helps to have knowledge of these controls so that you can be confident that that cash sale data you are recording is accurate.

 brilliant recap

- Cash receipts are recorded in a cash receipts book.
- If a business receives a lot of cash (notes and coins) and makes payments from this cash before banking it, a cash book can be used to show these payments.
- A cheque payments book records all cash that leaves the bank, be it by cheque, direct debit, etc.
- A reconciliation between the bank balance in the business books and the bank statement is a very important book-keeping task.
- If a business handles higher volumes of cash, it may be necessary for the book-keeper or owner to have additional checks and controls in place.

CHAPTER 6

Keeping track of employees

As a book-keeper or business owner, it is likely that you'll have to keep track of monies due to and/or paid to employees. This may be particularly so in a smaller business, where the book-keeper or owner is responsible for recruiting and paying staff.

You should avoid doing payroll (i.e. paying staff) manually, and this includes using spreadsheets. The taxation systems in most countries are anything but simple and require detailed knowledge of rules and relevant laws. The best thing to do is to get some payroll software, which you might find can be obtained free if the number of employees is small. You'll get a brief introduction to one free piece of UK payroll software later in this chapter. An alternative to software is to outsource the preparation of wages to a payroll bureau, which you might find in your locality or even online.

Having employees means more than just paying your staff. There are many legal requirements that need to be considered, most of which are often seen as a burden by small businesses in particular. Quite often, the book-keeper may be responsible for many payroll and employee-related matters, so in this chapter you'll learn the basic tasks a book-keeper might encounter.

Hiring staff

Normally, a book-keeper is not involved in the recruitment process, but if you're in business as a sole trader, you may have to do the recruiting if the business is growing. Having said that, a book-keeper generally is seen as a suitable person to keep records in any business, so they quite often deal with some tasks after the decision to employ a new member of staff is made.

The first thing any new employee should receive is the terms and conditions of employment. These include things like the rate of pay, holiday entitlements, disciplinary procedures, etc. They are normally written into a 'Contract of Employment', which is signed by the new employee and the employer. There may also be requirements to inform new employees of the health and safety policy. These things often can be complex, so if you are unsure of the requirements for your business, do ask for help from the relevant government agencies.

brilliant tip

For things like contracts of employment or safety policy statements, you don't need to start from scratch. Ask someone you know who has already done one for a loan of their documents, and use them as a guide or template.

Now for the more typical book-keeping tasks related to new staff. First, we need to know how much income tax to deduct from the employee each week or month. This information normally is given on a form issued by the previous employer, if there is one. In the UK, this form is called a P45. The form provides the new employer with personal details (such as tax and/or national insurance reference number), earnings for the year thus far, date of leaving the previous job and the cumulative taxation deducted. As a new employer, you need to ask the employee for their P45. You should then complete the relevant sections and forward them to the local tax office, which will, in turn, inform you of the allowances/ credits applicable to a new employee. If you employ someone who has not worked previously or for a long while, they might need to get a new tax reference number and/or apply for tax allowances. This is something the employee themselves will have to sort out.

Once you have previous tax details from the P45 and know the rates of pay for the employee, you can then enter their details into the payroll software and calculate the pay due. So let's see what kind of things you may need to do to get your payroll done.

Running the payroll

As mentioned earlier in this chapter, your best bet is to get some payroll software to do your payroll. But first let's get an appreciation of how a payroll system might work. 'Payroll system' means all tasks to complete a weekly or monthly payroll – software is just one part of this.

Pay elements

Pay elements is a term used to describe the components of pay a member of staff receives. The most common pay element is a standard hourly rate of pay. This is usually called 'basic pay' and is the amount paid per hour to employees who work on an hourly basis. You probably know that basic pay applies to what might be termed a 'normal' day or week. This means that if an employee works more than the agreed normal hours, then additional pay may be given. Additional pay might be at 1.5 times the normal hourly rate, double or even triple the rate. The rate of pay beyond normal hours should be written in the terms and conditions of employment to avoid confusion.

There are many other possible pay elements. Some of the more common ones are listed below.

● An individual or group bonus – this is usually performance-related, e.g. meeting a particular output target.
● Commission on sales – for example, a salesperson may be paid a low basic rate of pay plus a commission on sales at an agreed percentage.
● A monthly fixed salary – this is more often the form of pay given to managerial or administrative staff. It is fixed each month, regardless of hours worked.

It is also possible that staff can be paid on the basis of output rather than time. This is called a 'piece-rate' system.

 **example**

Employees in the agricultural and horticultural sectors often are paid using a piece-rate system. For example, mushroom growers pay staff by the weight of mushrooms harvested. Paying in this way ensures mushrooms are harvested at a good pace. If paid by the hour, it might be more difficult to motivate staff to harvest enough.

Recording the work done

Whether employees are paid based on time or an output measure, a system is needed to record the work done. This is often the job of the book-keeper, so let's see some methods often used. The one common factor in all these methods is that the employee is not left with full control of recording their own time or output. The reason for this is the obvious possibility of manipulation.

Recording time worked

In the vast majority of businesses, employees are paid on an hourly basis and, therefore, recording the hours worked is the first step in getting the payroll done. The most common way to collect hours worked is to use some form of time clock. Traditionally, employees used a time clock and a personalised punch-card to record the time they started and left work. Nowadays, the basic idea is the same but the device used is more likely to be a swipe card. Recording time worked in this way prevents manipulation of the hours by employees. In a smaller business, employees might sign in or simply be monitored by someone else, e.g. the owner.

Once the hours worked have been recorded, they become an input for the payroll. However, there are a number of things you need to watch out for before starting to work out the pay. These are as follows:

- Is a grace period allowed? For example, an employee might be allowed to be a maximum of 15 minutes late before suffering any loss of pay. In a company I worked for in the past, if you were any more than 15 minutes late you lost an hour's pay.
- Were additional or overtime hours worked? Can these be isolated separately? You need to be able to identify the hours worked at the applicable overtime rates, e.g. time and a half, double time.
- Was the employee ill? If so, are they to be paid?
- Is supervisor or manager approval needed for any additional hours worked?

Once matters such as these have been dealt with, the hours are ready for use in calculating the pay due. Now we need to consider any other forms of pay employees might get.

Capturing other pay elements

Earlier, examples of other pay elements such as a salesperson's commissions or employee bonuses were mentioned. Another obvious pay element is a fixed salary, which more often is associated with managers or administration staff. Other examples might be travel allowances, tool allowances (often given to construction employees), etc. The number of possible pay elements is vast, so it's impossible to mention them all in this chapter. The key point is to have a system to ensure you are aware of the pay elements for each employee and to find a way to incorporate them into the payroll. Here's an example.

> the key point is to have a system to ensure you are aware of the pay elements for each employee

 **example**

Your company employs two sales staff. They both have a small fixed salary and are paid a commission based on a percentage of sales. They are paid monthly. Jot down in the space below where you would best find the information needed for the payroll.

_____

_____

_____

_____

The fixed salary per month should be available from the contract of employment for each salesperson. If you don't have these, ask the relevant person for this information. The percentage commission on sales should also be available with the terms of employment. Finally, the sales figure is available from either your sales day book (you might have to total by customer) or your accounting software. You can then calculate the commission due. With this information, you now are ready to calculate the pay for the sales staff.

So before you start to calculate pay, you need to have all hours worked and/or other pay elements available. Now let's look at the basic principles of calculating pay.

Calculating pay

As you may know already, pay is subject to taxes and social insurance on the employee's part. As an employer, there are normally additional considerations such as an employer's contribution to social insurance. Tax and social insurance regulations can be quite complex and that's why it is a good idea for any book-keeper seriously to consider using payroll software. Additionally, tax and social insurance differ vastly from country to country. In this chapter, detailed information on tax and social insurance rates is not given, rather an overview of how the systems work. This is sufficient knowledge to get you started with any payroll software.

As already mentioned, the first thing is to have all pay elements at hand, e.g. hours worked, monthly salary, bonus, commission, etc. If you use payroll software, most of this kind of information can be stored on the employee's record. Only items that vary each pay period need to be input, e.g. hours worked each week. With this information you now have the gross pay for each employee.

 brilliant definition

> *Gross pay* is the payment due to an employee before deductions such as taxes, social insurance, health insurance, etc. *Net pay* refers to the amount of pay remaining after all deductions or, in other words, the 'take-home pay'.

Once the gross pay has been calculated, various deductions are made to arrive at the net pay. There are numerous possible deductions from pay, the most obvious being tax and social insurance. Here are some examples of other possible deductions:

- Pension – some employers offer a personal pension scheme whereby regular amounts are deducted from the employee and paid to a pension fund.
- Health insurance – in a similar way to pensions, some employers offer private health insurance schemes to employees. Again, regular deductions are made from the pay of the employee.
- Trade union subscriptions – where employees are trade union members, the subscription usually is deducted from their wages.

- Social or sports clubs – some employers organise social activities for their staff or fund a sports club. This usually requires a small deduction from employees towards the costs.

- Savings schemes or staff loans – deductions can be made to repay an employee loan or to pay into a staff savings scheme.

- Share purchase schemes – some large companies offer shares in the company to staff, making deductions from pay to cover the cost of the shares.

Whatever the deduction from pay, the book-keeper normally will have to keep track of the paying over of these deductions to the relevant party. For example, tax and social insurance are usually paid monthly to the tax authorities. It is a good idea to pay over regularly all deductions, because if you don't they can mount up and might cause cash-flow problems. So write a cheque each month to the pension company, trade union, social club or whatever.

Tax and social insurance are the two deductions you will have for all employees. Let's have a quick look at how these deductions are worked out. The figures used in the examples here are based around the UK's Pay As You Earn (PAYE) income tax system. The PAYE system means that tax is deducted from employees' pay each week or month, rather than paid over at the end of a year. The following example should be considered only as a demonstration of the principles of how tax is calculated. As the tax rules change frequently and depend on the circumstances of the individual, you would have to change the figures in the example to get the right tax amount.

brilliant example

Let's assume an employee earns £500 gross pay per week. The employee is entitled to £6,475 personal allowance per annum. This means they can earn £6,475 per annum before paying tax, or £124.60 per week. The income tax rate is 20%.

The tax to be deducted is calculated as follows:

(Gross pay – tax allowances) X rate of tax

The tax to be deducted will be thus £375.40 (£500 – £124.60) × 20%, or £75.08.

Social insurance (called National Insurance (NI) in the UK) is calculated as a percentage of gross pay, but some of the pay usually is exempt from National Insurance. The 2009–2010 rate of National Insurance is 11% on weekly earnings between £110 and £844. In addition, the employer pays National Insurance at the rate of 12.8% of gross pay above £110. This is not a deduction from the employee's pay, but must be paid to the tax authorities by the employer.

brilliant example

Using the same gross pay as in the previous example, the National Insurance would be calculated as follows:

Employee's NI = £500 − £110 = £390 × 11% = £42.90

Employer's NI = £500 − £110 = £390 × 12.8% = £49.92

Using these figures and the previous example, the net pay for the employee would be £500 − £75.08 (PAYE) − £42.90 (NI) = £382.02

The total PAYE and NI to be paid to the tax authorities is as follows:

	£
PAYE	75.08
NI – employee	42.90
NI – employer	49.92
Total due	167.90

In a similar way to paying over VAT, the employer must pay these amounts on a monthly or quarterly basis. On an annual basis, employers must provide full details of pay, PAYE and NI deductions itemised by employee using two forms called P14 and P35.

You can see there is a lot of work associated with payroll. The complexities of the tax and social insurance systems only compound the work. So always use payroll software. There is some free software available for UK payroll, so let's look briefly at one now. The advantage of using software is that you need only enter the employee's details and the pay elements and it will do the tax and social insurance calculations for you.

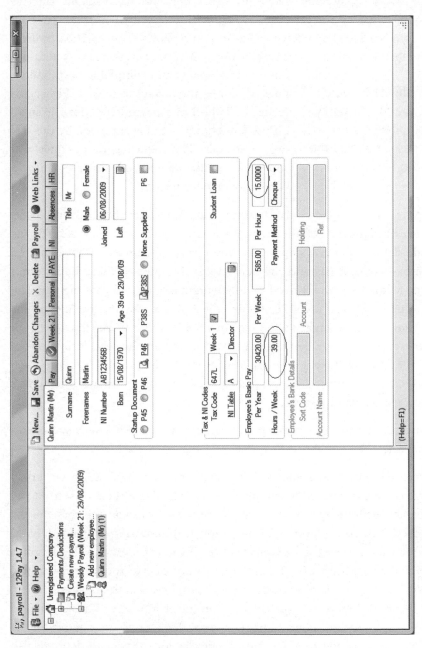

Figure 6.1 Employee details in 12Pay

The software used here is called 12Pay, which has a free version available from www.12pay.co.uk. There are other free options available, such as Payroo (www.payroo.com) or PayThyme (www.paythyme.org.uk), or paid options like Sage Payroll, which has several versions costing £100 upwards. Whether you use free software or buy some, the key things to watch out for are functionality and compliance with guidelines set out by the tax authorities. 12Pay seems to have all the basic payroll functions a small business might need and is approved by the UK tax authorities. The following figures give you some idea of how any payroll software can help you easily manage payroll.

> the key things to watch out for are functionality and compliance with guidelines set out by the tax authorities

Figure 6.1 shows the kind of basic information needed for each employee. The essential pieces of information are names, start date, date of birth, tax code, NI number and pay details. You can see (encircled) I have entered the basic rate of pay and the normal weekly hours. If these hours don't change, then you don't need to do anything else to calculate the pay. The tax code is shown as 647L. Under the UK tax system, this means the employee has a standard allowance of £6,475 and is under the age of 65. Different codes may be required based on the employee's circumstances and, of course, taxation systems in other countries may not use such codes. Nevertheless, the basic principle of a portion of income being free from tax generally applies.

Now let's see how the week's pay is calculated. Figure 6.2 shows a screen-shot where the pay for week number 21 has been calculated.

You can see that the standard hours (39) and rate of pay (£15 per hour) have come across from the employee's records. There is also a second pay element for holiday pay of £100. Underneath, you can see that the tax and NI deductions (employer and employee) have been calculated. Have a look back at the earlier examples to see if you can work out these figures manually (you might be a penny or two out due to rounding). Pay will be calculated in a similar manner for all employees in the business. Then, as shown in Figure 6.3, the software produces a payslip. This is given to each employee and shows all pay elements, deductions and net pay for the week/month in question. Cumulative figures for the year-to-date are also normally shown on a payslip.

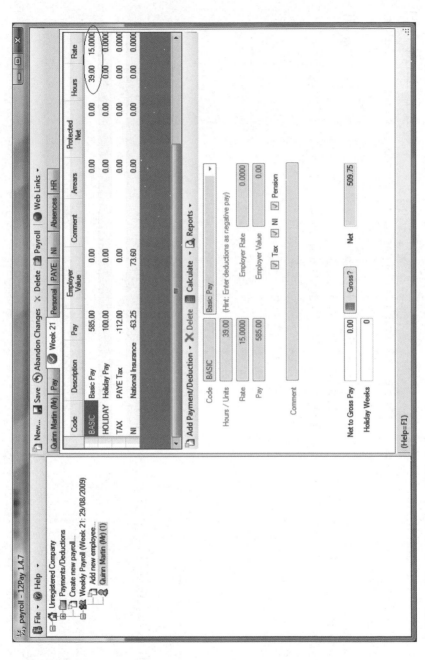

Figure 6.2 Payroll calculation in 12Pay

Unregistered Company

Quinn Martin (Mr)

Pay Date	Week	Tax Code	NI Table	NI Number	Department	Employee Number	Method
29 August 2009	21	647L/1	A	AB123456B		1	Cheque

Payments

	Pay	Tax	NI
Basic Pay: 39 @ £15.00	585.00	Y	Y
Holiday Pay	100.00	Y	Y

Total Payments 685.00

Deductions

	Pay	Tax	NI
PAYE Tax	112.00		
National Insurance	63.25		

Total Deductions 175.25

Net Pay 509.75

	Taxable Pay	Tax	NIable Pay	NI	Er's NI
Current Week	685.00	112.00	685.00	63.25	73.60
This Employment	685.00	112.00	685.00	63.25	73.60

Figure 6.3 Employee payslip from 12Pay

The advantages of payroll software are quite obvious, the greatest being removing the complex calculations. It's still a good idea to have a basic understanding of how a payroll system works manually, so you can at least double-check anything odd that might occur in software. Software also saves a lot of time compared with doing manual payroll. If you can't break away from your manual books for sales, purchases, etc., do so without hesitation for payroll. It really does save time and provides you with accurate payroll without the need for a detailed knowledge of tax and social insurance regulations. And finally, as the tax and social insurance rules can change frequently (at least once per year), if you do use software be sure to keep your software up to date.

Recording pay in the day books

When the pay has been calculated, employees are paid their net pay in cash, by cheque or most likely by bank transfer. The net pay is paid each week, fortnight or month depending on how often employees are paid. As mentioned, taxes and social insurance usually are paid over to the tax authorities each month. It's always a good idea to pay over any deductions such as trade union fees or pension deductions each month too.

Therefore, even if the book-keeper is not involved with payroll, all payments coming from the payroll need to be captured in the cheque payments book or accounting software. The net pay would be recorded each pay period in the cheque payments book, with payments of taxes and other deductions recorded as they are paid over. These payments will of course find their way to the nominal ledger. The wages account will increase, the bank account will decrease and the deductions accounts (taxes, etc.) will decrease when paid.

Employee expenses

Many businesses cover the expenses of employees who are required to work off-site or travel a lot. These expenses usually are paid back to employees on a regular basis. As book-keeper, even if you don't do the payroll, you might still be responsible for a system to collate, approve and pay employee expenses. In small businesses, such a system is probably manual, with only large companies using specialised expense tracking software to manage employee expenses.

Expense Claim

Claim Number:

Purpose: _____

Employee Information

Name _____   Department _____
NI Number _____   Position _____
Employee ID _____ Manager _____

Pay Period
From _____
To _____

Date	Account	Description	Hotel	Transport	Fuel	Meals	Phone	Entertainment	Misc.	TOTAL
									£	£ -
									£	£ -
									£	£ -
									£	£ -
									£	£ -
									£	£ -
									£	£ -
									£	£ -
									£	£ -
			£ -	£ -	£ -	£ -	£ -	£ -	£ -	

Subtotal £
Advances £
TOTAL £ -

Approved _____   Notes _____

Figure 6.4 Sample employee expense claim form

There are many ways to manage employee expenses, but there are two key ways to approach expenses. First, you can give employees money to spend in advance and then ask them to produce receipts to cover the money spent. Second, employees themselves can pay for the expenses and are then reimbursed on production of receipts. The former is similar to a petty cash system (see Chapter 4), whereby money is given in advance, run down, and then topped up as necessary. If employee expenses are quite small and infrequent, this system might be fine. The latter system is more common and is used in this chapter. Whichever system is used, it is very important to have a system in place. This is because tax authorities will view any payment to employees as income (i.e. wages) unless supporting evidence of expenses can be produced. If treated as income, employees would be liable for income tax, which of course would not be fair for the employee.

Expense claim forms

Probably the best way to record and manage employee expenses is to use an expense claim form. Such a form is used by employees to claim back monies they have already spent in the course of their work. You can use Microsoft Excel or another spreadsheet to draw up a usable claim form easily. Figure 6.4 shows an example, which is in fact based upon an in-built template provided within Excel.

This sample (Figure 6.4) is quite typical and looks a little like a cheque payments book. The headings would of course be determined by your business, with the basic idea being to capture and analyse each expense. The top portion of the form is used to complete the employee's staff details and reasons for the expenses. Using a spreadsheet like Excel can be quite handy as you can distribute a template like the one in Figure 6.4 to all employees. They in turn can fill out the personal details once and save it.

Each expense on a claim form should be supported by a receipt. Apply this policy quite strictly as this keeps employees conscious of the need to produce receipts and, more importantly, prevents any issues with the tax authorities.

each expense on a claim form should be supported by a receipt

On receiving a new expense claim, the book-keeper should follow a number of steps as follows:

- Ensure the purpose of the expense claim is solely for the business.
- If the expense claim is completed by hand, do a quick check to ensure all figures are right.
- Ensure each line has been analysed in an expense category, e.g. hotel, meals, travel, etc.
- Ensure each item is accompanied by a valid receipt.
- Give the claim a number, usually a sequential number, so that it can be filed and referred to.
- If expense claims are to be authorised by an employee's manager or department head, seek the correct authorisation.
- Pay the claim without delay once authorisation has been granted.
- Record the payment appropriately, in the cheque payments book or your accounting software. Use the claim number as a reference. The analysis headings on the expense claim are your guide to how to analyse the payment too.

These are good guidelines, but of course you can vary them depending on your business. For example, you could decide that an employee has a £5 per day lunch allowance for which you don't require receipts. In general, though, seek receipts for the majority of expenses.

brilliant recap

- Payroll can be a complex and time-consuming exercise for the book-keeper. Use software if you can.

- Pay elements refer to the type of pay an employee receives, e.g. basic pay, overtime pay, bonus pay, sales commission, etc. All elements need to be recorded.

- The sum of all pay elements is referred to as gross pay.

- Deductions such as taxation, social insurance, pension, trade union fees, etc. are taken from gross pay to arrive at net pay.

- Taxes and/or social insurance deducted from pay must be paid over to the tax authorities on a regular basis. Even if the book-keeper does not do the payroll, the payroll figures need to be recorded in the day books.

- A system should be in place to record and pay any expenses incurred by employees in the course of their work.

CHAPTER 7

Recording and tracking assets

This chapter looks at some additional book-keeping work which is often necessary to keep track of the assets of a business. You'll learn first about non-current assets and then about stocks (inventories). The work described in this chapter will also be referred to in Chapters 9 and 10.

The amount of work a book-keeper will have to do on non-current assets and stock will depend on the type of business. For example, a manufacturing business is more likely to have lots more equipment (non-current assets) than a recruitment agency. Nonetheless, the principles to record and track the assets will be similar.

Recording non-current assets

What are non-current assets?

In Chapter 1, you learned what an asset is. Here is the definition again, to remind you.

 brilliant definition

An *asset* is something that is owned or something to which you have rights, that will deliver a benefit, and for which costs can be readily determined.

Non-current assets, which are often called fixed or tangible assets, refer to assets that are held for a number of years and have a productive use, i.e. they are used to help realise profits. A business might have a premises, office equipment, machinery, etc., all of which are non-current assets. As already noted in Chapter 2, a business need not necessarily have full legal ownership of an asset for it to be considered an asset in accounting terms.

The asset register

'Asset register' is a term used to describe a system that records and tracks the non-current assets of a business. It is used not only by accountants but also by engineers, maintenance staff, insurance companies, etc. who need information on the cost, location and condition of the non-current assets of a business. Most businesses have a policy of what they regard as a non-current asset, and thus something that is recorded on the asset register. Such a policy might be centred on how material the asset is relative to the business. For example, the purchase of a single laptop for £400 might be regarded as an expense rather than an asset, whereas the simultaneous purchase of 50 such laptops (£20,000) would be more material and would be recorded in the asset register – or, in other words, treated as capital expenditure.

In Figure 7.1, I outline some details that an asset register might contain. The requirements will vary by business, depending on factors like business size, number of locations, etc.

Nature of asset	Details of the asset, e.g. date of purchase, cost, movability, serial number/tracking number
Disclosure requirements	Details of any rules or regulations that might apply to the business and/or asset. For example, reports on noise emissions or hazardous substances associated with the assets
Ownership	Is the asset owned or on lease?
Insurance requirements	Any specific requirements for insurance on the asset, e.g. additional security/control procedures
Location	The normal location(s) of the asset
Maintenance	This portion of an asset register might be used by engineers or maintenance staff to track regular servicing of assets, e.g. date of last service
Depreciation method	This details how the cost of the asset is spread over its useful life (see later)

Figure 7.1 Contents of an asset register

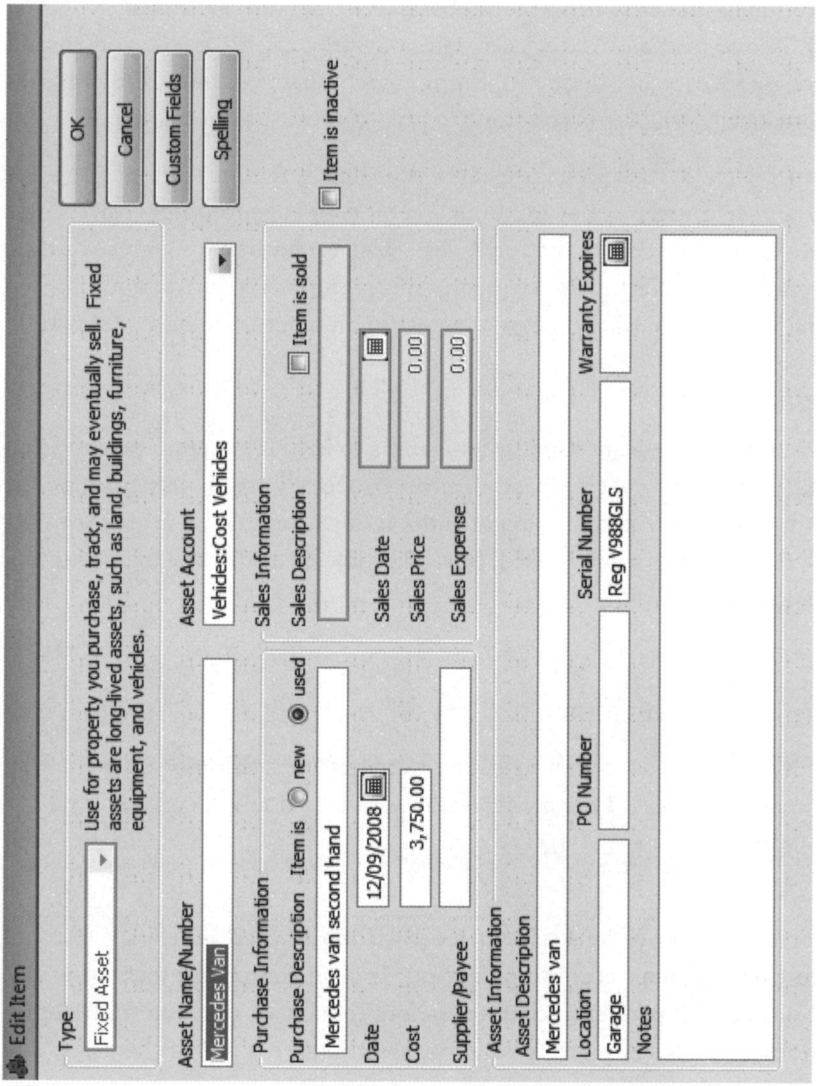

Figure 7.2 Recording a non-current asset in QuickBooks

Smaller businesses may use a simple spreadsheet to prepare an asset register, e.g. Microsoft Excel has several useful templates available to help you. Larger businesses are more likely to use software, which may or may not be part of their accounting software. QuickBooks does offer some functionality which records basic asset details (as shown in Figure 7.2) like the purchase date, sales date, warranty expiry, etc. If you enter a purchase invoice or cheque to a non-current asset account, QuickBooks automatically will ask if you want to record these additional details.

From Figure 7.1, you can see that recording assets in the asset register serves many purposes beyond book-keeping and accounting. However, as book-keeper or accountant you will be concerned mainly with recording the cost of an asset and subsequently spreading this cost over a number of years. This notion of spreading the cost of an asset is called depreciation.

Depreciation

Non-current assets are used by a business to help it generate revenue and make profits, but over a period of time. A delivery truck may be good for five or more years and you might think it is reasonable to spread the cost over the years the truck is used. Spreading the cost this way in accounting is called depreciation.

 brilliant definition

Depreciation is an accounting technique used to spread the cost of non-current assets over a number of years, usually referred to as the useful life of the asset.

Depreciation apportions part of the cost of a non-current asset that has been used up in an accounting period. It is an estimating technique and will not be 100 per cent accurate. Before looking at two common depreciation methods, let's clarify what we mean by the 'cost' of the asset. The cost will include the purchase price of the asset, but other initial costs should also be included, as shown in the following example.

brilliant example

A manufacturing business purchases a new piece of machinery from Germany for £1 million. The cost of transport is £50,000. In addition, engineers need to spend two weeks setting up the new machine at a cost of £60,000. The cost of the machine thus would be £1.1 million in the asset register.

Accounting rules state that all costs to get an asset to a workable or useable condition should be included. So, for example, if your business buys a building, any associated legal costs would be included in the asset cost. Additionally, substantial modifications to existing assets should be recorded in the asset register. For example, if the machine referred to in the example needed to have a motor replaced, the cost of the new motor would be included and the cost of the old replaced motor would be taken off the register.

Depreciation methods

The two most common methods of estimating depreciation are known as the straight-line method and the reducing-balance method. Both methods

	£
Cost of asset	22,000
Residual value	1,000
Estimated life	6 years
Depreciation per annum	
Cost – residual value =	21,000
Useful life	6
Annual depreciation =	3,500

Figure 7.3 Straight-line depreciation method

have the objective of spreading the cost of an asset over a number of years. The concept is in fact an application of the accruals concept. Let's see the straight-line method first. Figure 7.3 shows how this method works.

As the name suggests, the straight-line method assumes that an asset provides benefits evenly over its useful life and thus the cost should be spread evenly. In this example, the residual (or scrap) value is deducted from the cost as this amount reflects what the asset might be sold for after six years and this reduces the overall cost. You can see that using this method, the annual depreciation is £3,500. This amount is recorded as an expense.

Figure 7.4 shows the reducing-balance method for the same asset. With this method, the depreciation charge is based on the reduced balance (cost minus depreciation to date). This means a higher depreciation charge occurs in earlier years.

	£
Cost of asset	22,000
Depreciation to be 20%	
of reduced balance	
Year 1 depreciation	4,400
Year 1 reduced balance	17,600
Year 2 depreciation	
(20% of £17,600)	3,520
Year 2 reduced balance	14,080
Year 3 depreciation	
(20% of £14,080)	2,816
Year 3 reduced balance	11,264
(and so on...)	

Figure 7.4 Reducing-balance depreciation method

The question is, which depreciation method do you use? The best answer is to think about how the asset actually provides benefits to the business. If benefits are pretty equal, or the wear and tear is equal each year, then the straight-line method might be best. For example, buildings and office furniture often are depreciated using this method. When assets become less efficient as they get older, the reducing-balance method is often used. Motor vehicles and machinery are often depreciated using this method.

There are no rules dictating exactly how each asset should be depreciated, i.e. over how many years or what percentage per annum. However, accounting rules do say that all assets of the same class should be depreciated consistently. So, in other words, if you depreciate a motor vehicle over five years using the straight-line method, you must do this for all motor vehicles.

The depreciation calculated for each year is an expense. The accumulated depreciation over the years is recorded in the balance sheet and set against the original cost of the asset – the resulting figure is called net book value. In Chapter 9, you'll learn how depreciation features in the financial statements.

Keeping track of stocks

If a business buys (or makes) and sells products, it is likely to hold a stock of these goods. The term stock applies to items that are either available for sale or are components which are assembled to make products. Generally, the stocks in a business can fall into three categories as follows:

1 **Raw material stock**   If a business manufactures products, it is likely to hold stocks of the materials needed to make the products.

2 **Work-in-progress**   This refers to products that are partially complete. For example, in a computer manufacturer like Dell, there will always be some unfinished computers at the end of a day or shift.

3 **Finished goods stock**   This refers to items that are fully complete and ready for sale. These may be items a business has either made or bought in.

Stocks are often referred to as inventory – there is no difference in the meaning of the words, but you may find the term inventory used in larger businesses. As stocks are an asset of a business and quite often have a considerable monetary value, a business normally will have a system to record items coming in, items sold and thus items remaining in stock.

The type of system a business uses to keep track of stock will depend on a number of factors, including the following:

● The size of the business – smaller businesses may use manual records. Stock cards, for example, are often used. These are simply a piece of card or paper showing all movements of stock – receipts, usage, breakages, etc. Larger businesses typically will use a software-based system.

- The value of the items – a common-sense approach is often taken whereby items of a higher value are recorded and tracked in a stock system, whereas low-value items are not. For example, a maintenance workshop might not bother to track items like screws or nuts and bolts, but will keep accurate records of spare machine parts which could be quite expensive.

- The 'walkability' factor – OK, this might not be a real word, but sometimes items held in stock in a business have a funny capability of 'walking' or, put another way, going missing. Such items might be small, desirable and relatively expensive, and thus subject to being stolen by staff, customers or the public.

brilliant example

You may have noticed in your local supermarket in recent years that products like Gillette razors (Mach 3 and Fusion ranges) are sold in plastic radio-tagged containers. This simply is due to the fact that these products are small, expensive and easy to conceal. They once were the most pilfered item in Europe. Thus retailers needed a simple, cost-effective solution to safeguard their stock of these items.

The goal of any stock system is two-fold: 1. to provide information on the quantity and location of items and 2. to put a value on the total amount of goods in stock. The remainder of this chapter examines how a business can keep track of items coming into the business, items going out and how to put a value on the stock. We'll use screenshots from QuickBooks to show you how accounting software can save a lot of time tracking stock. As you read on, you'll appreciate quickly that manual records of items moving in and out of a business can be cumbersome. Most businesses do rely on computerised records to track and value stock. Think of retailers like Tesco or Sainsbury which have thousands of products, all of which must be tracked. You probably notice that as you do your shopping in supermarkets such as these, everything is scanned. Not only does this capture the sale (Chapter 3), it also updates the amount in stock. OK, most businesses are not as complex as the large retailers, but a goal of any business with substantial stocks should be to limit the manual input in recording and tracking items.

> limit the manual input in recording and tracking items

Stocks coming into the business

In Chapter 4, the recording of purchases was examined in some detail. You will remember that the source documents for purchases are suppliers' invoices. These invoices contain details of the items bought, which may be items the business needs to keep in stock and keep track of. Thus, the purchase invoices could be used as a source of information for stock coming into a business. In a small business, this might be the easiest way, particularly when the volume of items held in stock is quite small. Typically, in such a business the book-keeper might check that goods on the invoice were received. There is also an additional source document which was not mentioned in earlier chapters – a delivery docket. This document should be given to a business when goods are delivered – this is often long before the invoice for the goods arrives. Thus, when items are delivered the best thing to do is check the goods against the delivery docket. This fulfils two functions: 1. the quantity delivered is verified and 2. if there are any discrepancies the supplier can be notified.

As book-keeper, you might be involved in recording stock movements in or out of the business, but it is more likely that someone else will do the inputting. For example, a stores person might record the goods coming in. Your role as book-keeper might be to check delivery dockets against invoices before paying suppliers – you might check quantities, for example. You might also have a role in a previous step, which is ordering goods from suppliers, although this can also be done by stores people or even a central purchasing function. Orders to suppliers are written in a document called a purchase order, which in accounting software like QuickBooks normally is the first source of data for the stock management features. Take a look at Figure 7.5, which shows a purchase order from Sample Port Meadow Locksmiths in QuickBooks.

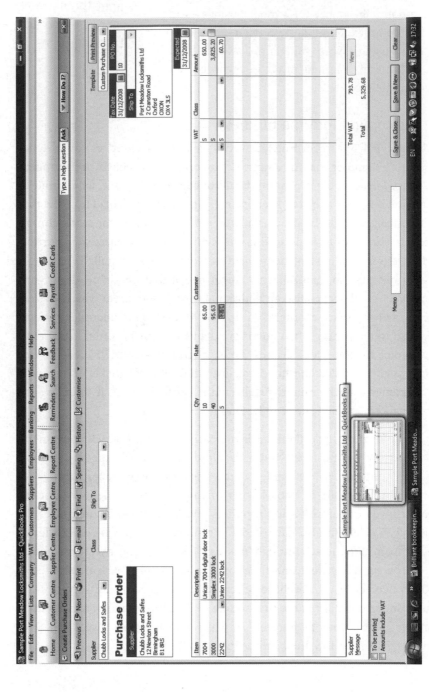

Figure 7.5 A purchase order in QuickBooks

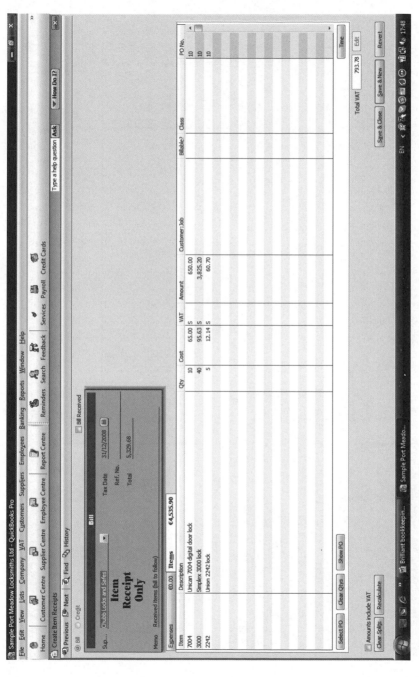

Figure 7.6 Receiving goods in QuickBooks

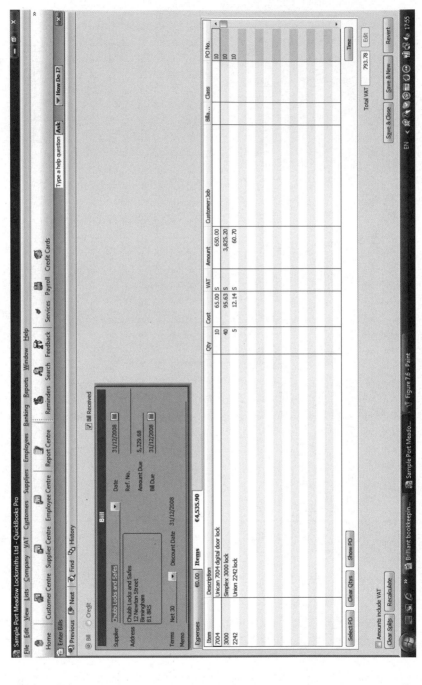

Figure 7.7 Entering a bill against goods received in QuickBooks

In the purchase order in Figure 7.5, you can see an order to a supplier called Chubb Locks and Safes for three types of lock. The quantity and price of each is listed, as is the total value. This purchase order would be sent to the supplier, who would then deliver the goods. Once the goods are received, the receipt is also recorded, as shown in Figure 7.6, by simply calling up a 'Received Goods' option. This option traces the purchase order back to the supplier and needs minimal data input. The quantities can be changed at this point but, if the quantity received is the same as ordered, you need only accept and save the receipt.

In Figure 7.6, you'll see the words 'Item Receipt Only' at the top left. This means that the supplier's invoice is to follow. This normally would be the case. First, suppliers deliver goods, with the customer (you) signing a delivery docket. This delivery docket then becomes proof that you accepted the goods and is used by the supplier to prepare their invoice. Some companies don't do delivery dockets nowadays and simply issue an invoice with the delivery. Let's assume that in our QuickBooks example the supplier's invoice comes later. Now take a look at Figure 7.7.

It looks a lot like Figure 7.6 except that we are now entering the bill (invoice) from the supplier for the goods already received. Looking at Figure 7.7 and back at Chapter 4 – Figure 4.3 (p. 53) in particular – you can see the links between a purchase order, a purchase invoice and keeping track of stock. If a business uses such functions in its accounting software, you can see it becomes a lot easier to record items of stock coming into a business.

The sequence of events depicted in Figures 7.5–7.7 is typical of how a business might track incoming items of stock. Of course, the volume and range of items held in stock will vary widely from business to business. If your business or the one you work in needs to track stock, then be sure to use software as it saves a lot of time and effort.

Selling or using stocks

In Chapter 3, the recording of sales of a business was detailed. Each sale of a product reduces the amount in stock, so the logical thing for a book-keeper or store person to do is to use the sales invoices as a basis for capturing stocks going out of a business.

> use the sales invoices as a basis for capturing stocks going out of a business

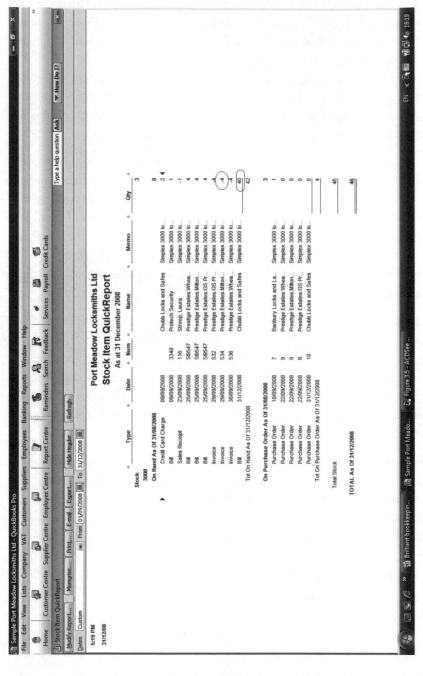

Figure 7.8 Stock status and history in QuickBooks

Look back at Figure 3.5 (p. 40) and you'll see that this sales invoice captured the sale of three items – the fourth item is a labour charge. The quantity of each item sold would reduce the quantity in stock. Now take a look at Figure 7.8.

In Figure 7.8 you can see a snapshot of the movements of one stock item which has featured in the previous examples, the 'Simplex 3000' lock (see Figures 3.5 and Figures 7.5–7.7). You'll see the sale of four of the 'Simplex 3000' locks (circled) to Prestige Estates as in the sales invoice shown in Figure 3.5 (p. 40). You can also see the 40 locks received in Figures 7.6 and 7.7.

You can see how easy it is to capture the movements (purchases and sales) of stocks when you use software. You can imagine the amount of paperwork this would involve! It makes a lot of sense to spend some time setting up software to manage stocks. It might take some time initially, but it saves a lot of time in the long run.

> it makes a lot of sense to spend some time setting up software to manage stocks

These examples assume that a business simply buys and sells products. If products are assembled or manufactured, managing and tracking stock becomes a little more difficult. This is because you have to distinguish between stock components used in the manufacturing process and stocks of completed products. The principles are exactly the same, but an added step of tracking materials or components issued to the production floor is required. This is similar to the tracking of sales shown here in that items used in the production reduce the stock. Tracking stocks of materials or components in a manufacturing or assembly operation is important not only for accounting and book-keeping purposes but also for production staff as they need to ensure enough stock is on hand to allow production to continue without delays.

Checking and valuing stocks

Normally a business will need to check and value its stocks at least once a year – at the end of the financial year. This is to obtain a value of the stocks for the balance sheet (see Chapter 9). As part of this process, an auditor may be present to verify that stocks exist and are counted correctly. Some businesses do stock takes on a more frequent basis. If accounting software is used, then, in theory at least, the amount and value of stock at any point in time should be readily available (see Figure 7.9).

So how do you value the stock of a business? First you need to do a stock (or inventory) count as already mentioned. Some tips on doing a good stock count are given below.

brilliant tips

Here are some tips to help you conduct a good inventory count:

● Pick a time when your business is very quiet, preferably closed.

● Count all items, regardless of location, age or condition.

● Take a note of any damaged items.

● If several people are involved, create a summary of all items.

● Put a value on all items.

If you use QuickBooks or some other accounting software you may be able to get a report of items in stock and use this as a basis for the count (see Figure 7.10). Any corrections would be noted, investigated and reflected in the system. Once you have a count of all items, the calculations can be done to determine the total stock value. As noted earlier in this chapter, the value of items often will determine the controls adopted. Thus, for example, low-value items might not be counted at all during a stock take, or at infrequent intervals. Higher-value items are likely to receive a lot more attention.

5:12 PM
31/12/08

Port Meadow Locksmiths Ltd
Stock Valuation Summary
As at 31 December 2008

Stock	Item Description	On Hand	Avg. Cost	Asset Value	% of Tot. As...	Sales Price	Retail Value	% of Tot. Re...
Stock								
2101	Union 5 lever deadl...	4	12.00	48.00	0.8%	19.50	78.00	0.9%
2242	Union 2242 lock	14	12.14	169.96	2.9%	18.02	252.28	2.8%
3000	Simplex 3000 lock	42	95.63	4,016.46	69%	147.13	6,179.46	69.8%
3C14	Chubb 3C14 deadlo...	7	10.12	70.84	1.2%	21.61	151.27	1.7%
3K70	Chubb Mortise Lock...	8	23.95	191.60	3.3%	38.95	311.60	3.5%
7004	Unican 7004 digital	18	65.00	1,170.00	20.1%	90.79	1,634.22	18.4%
77	Yale 77 lock with br...	6	15.03	90.18	1.5%	21.61	129.66	1.5%
85lux	Yale 85 Basslux lock	3	22.10	66.30	1.1%	40.68	122.04	1.4%
Total Stock		102		5,823.34	100.00%		8,858.53	100.00%
TOTAL		102		5,823.34	100.00%		8,858.53	100.00%

Figure 7.9 Stock valuation report from QuickBooks

5:13 PM

31/12/08

Port Meadow Locksmiths Ltd
Stock Take Worksheet
All Transactions

	Item Description	Pref Suppl...	On Hand	Physical Co...
Stock				
2101	Union 5 lever deadl...		4	
2242	Union 2242 lock		14	
3000	Simplex 3000 lock		42	
3C...	Chubb 3C14 deadlo...		7	
3K...	Chubb Mortise Lock...		8	
7004	Unican 7004 digital ...		18	
77	Yale 77 lock with br...		6	
85I...	Yale 85 Basslux lock		3	

Figure 7.10 A stock take sheet from QuickBooks

stocks are valued at the lower of cost or net realisable value

Accounting has a rule that stocks are valued at the lower of cost or net realisable value.

 brilliant definition

> In relation to stocks, *cost* means the amount for which the items were bought, including delivery charges, customs duties, etc. (but not VAT). *Net realisable value* means the sales value less any costs required to make the item saleable.

The net realisable value usually applies only to items that are damaged. For example, a furniture store might have a table that got scratched. It had cost £500, but can now be sold for only £450. Thus, its value is £450. The cost or net realisable value can be calculated for each individual item or groups of like items. Once determined, the cost or net realisable value simply is multiplied by the quantity of the items. All the numbers are added up and the resulting figure equals the total value of stock in a business.

In a manufacturing or assembly business, the principles of valuing stocks mentioned above apply to materials or components in stock and also to finished products. Additionally, a value must be put on work-in-progress.

brilliant definition

Work-in-progress refers to partially finished work in a manufacturing or contracting business. In accounting, a value needs to be put on this at the end of a financial year or accounting period.

If attempting to value work-in-progress, the cost is determined as all costs to bring a product to its present location and condition. This will include material/component costs, labour and other expenses. Mostly, an accountant will do this work using costs given by a book-keeper.

brilliant recap

- Non-current assets are recorded in an asset register. This register keeps details such as date of purchase, cost, location and depreciation method.

- Two common depreciation methods are: 1. the straight-line method and 2. the reducing-balance method.

- The depreciation methods used depend on the business and asset type. Each business can choose its depreciation method and, once chosen, this method should be applied consistently to similar assets.

- When a business has considerable volumes of items in stock, it is usual to have a stock control system.

- Stocks are valued for the purposes of preparing financial statements. The value is the lower of cost or net realisable value.

PART 3

From day books to financial statements

CHAPTER 8

Ledger accounts

Throughout earlier chapters, you will remember that transactions from the day books are in turn posted to ledger accounts. In this chapter, you'll learn the basics of ledger accounts. If you look back at Figure 1.1 (p. 5), you'll see that the ledgers are the next step in the accounting cycle once transactions have been recorded in the day books. A book-keeper may or may not have a role in the keeping of ledgers. Sometimes an accountant within a business has responsibility for the ledgers, or an external accountant prepares them at year-end. It is common, though, for book-keepers to have some involvement with the personal ledgers. These ledgers contain accounts for each supplier and customer and are similar to the lists of customer and supplier balances seen in Chapters 3 and 4.

Ledger accounts follow the double-entry system of accounting. By the end of this chapter you will have an appreciation of the double-entry system and be able to understand at least what accountants are talking about when they start mentioning words like 'debit' and 'credit'. The chapter starts with a brief history of the origins of double-entry accounting, followed by some examples to show how the system works. You'll then see how the ledger accounts are used to draft a simple report called a 'trial balance', which is a key accounting tool.

Whether or not you work with ledgers depends on the size of the business, with smaller businesses requiring book-keepers to do more work using ledgers. No matter what your role, a basic knowledge of ledger accounts will, at a minimum, help you converse with accountants.

a basic knowledge of ledger accounts will help you converse with accountants

The double-entry system

Written accounting records are some of the oldest surviving writings, dating back to circa 3300 BC. These early records were simple notations of wages paid, temple assets, and taxes and tributes to a king or pharaoh. What we know today as the double-entry system of accounting was written about first by an Italian monk called Luca Pacioli. In 1494 he published a book* that detailed the double-entry system still used today.

The core premise of the double-entry system is that all business transactions are recorded in an 'account'. Each account is a history of money values of a particular aspect of a business. For example, a purchases account would record all purchases-related transactions and a sales account would record all sales-related transactions. The system is called double entry as each transaction must be recorded in at least two accounts. In earlier chapters, for example, you'll have seen how a credit sale would increase the sales account and increase the debtor's account, so there are two accounts in this transaction.

Now let's see how to record transactions in ledger accounts. Of course, software like QuickBooks can do all the recording for us, but we do need to understand how the double-entry system works.

Layout of a ledger account

Figure 8.1 shows the layout of a double-entry account. Think of an account as splitting a page into two sides.

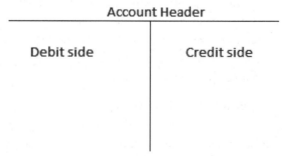

Figure 8.1 The layout of a double-entry account

*Summa de arithmetica, geometria, proportioni et proportionalita (Everything about arithmetic, geometry, and proportions).

The left-hand side of an account is called the 'debit' side, the right-hand side is called the 'credit' side. Each account has a header, which is just a name to help identify the account – for example, sales account, purchases account, office expenses account.

 **brilliant** tip

If you are referring to a ledger account, you can use the abbreviation a/c for account.

In addition to the fact that each business transaction is recorded in at least two accounts, there must be corresponding debit and credit entries. Accounts are written up in a 'ledger', which traditionally was a specialised hard-back book with two sides per page. You can use sheets of A4 paper, an analysis book, a spreadsheet or of course some accounting software. No matter what the format, the term ledger is still used to refer to where the accounts are written or stored.

How do I know which side of an account to use?

In Chapter 1, assets, liabilities, capital, revenue and expenditure were mentioned as key terms in the world of accounting and book-keeping. All these (assets, liabilities, etc.) are recorded in accounts in the ledger. To identify which one of the types of account applies in each transaction, there are some rules, as shown in Figure 8.2.

Account type	Debit	Credit
Asset	Increase	Decrease
Liability	Decrease	Increase
Capital	Decrease	Increase
Revenue	Decrease	Increase
Expenditure	Increase	Decrease

Figure 8.2 Rules for which side of a ledger account to use

To help you remember these rules, Figure 8.2 can be summarised as follows: if an asset is to be increased (e.g. the purchase of a new asset) you debit the asset account, whereas to decrease an asset you credit the asset account. The same rules apply to expenditure: liabilities, capital and revenue use the opposite – increases are credited.

Now that you have the rules, let's see how a business transaction would be reflected in a ledger account. Have a look back at Figure 3.3 (p. 35). On 1 October a sale of £1,050 to Great Doors Ltd was made. This was a net sale of £1,000 plus £50 VAT. First, ask yourself, what accounts do you think might be used in this transaction? Write down in the space below the three accounts you think are involved here.

The answers. There is an account for sales, an account for Great Doors Ltd and an account for VAT. Sales (referring to Figure 8.2) would be credited as sales increase. The account for Great Doors Ltd will be debited as it represents an asset (the customer owes us money) and the asset is increasing. Finally, the VAT account is a liability (we owe it to the tax authorities), is thus increased and is credited. Figure 8.3 shows the accounts written up.

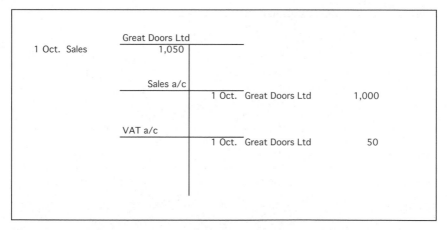

Figure 8.3 Recording a sale in ledger accounts

On each side of each account the transaction has a reference with the date and includes some other reference to link the transaction to the other accounts, i.e. the name of the other account. You should always try to do this, as it helps anyone trying to follow the transactions in the ledger. As you'll see shortly, software like QuickBooks will put in comments for us automatically.

Here's another example. In Figure 5.7 (p. 80), a direct debit payment for the telephone was made on 8 October for £120. Again ask yourself what accounts are involved, and write the two accounts in the space below.

1

2

The answers. This time the accounts are telephone and bank. Telephone is an expense, is being increased and is thus debited. Bank is an asset, is being decreased and is credited. Figure 8.4 shows the two accounts.

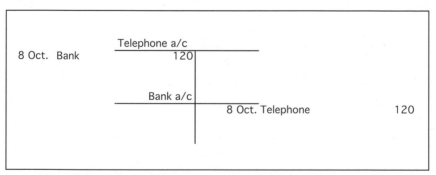

Figure 8.4 Payments in a ledger account

If you refer back to Figure 8.2, you will be able to put each account entry on the correct side of the accounts each time.

 **tip**

There is a phrase often used to learn double-entry rules: 'debit the receiver, credit the giver'. In Figure 8.3 Great Doors Ltd 'receives', sales 'gives'. In Figure 8.4, telephone 'receives', bank 'gives'.

Closing off a ledger account

Now you know how to record business transactions in a ledger account. No matter how complex the transaction, the same rules always apply.

As transactions occur, a history of the asset, expense, liability, etc. is built up in its account. Later in this chapter and in Chapter 9, we'll see that ledger accounts are the basis for the financial statement of a business. The first step in preparing financial statements is to 'close off' the ledger accounts. This means that a snapshot of the total value of each ledger account is taken at a point in time, usually a month-end or year-end. Closing off accounts is quite simple, all you need do is a little adding and subtracting.

Take a look at Figure 8.5. This shows the ledger account of AB Supplies Ltd. The transactions recorded are those shown earlier in the purchases day book (Figure 4.1, p. 50) and the cheque payments book (Figure 5.7, p. 80).

		AB Supplies Ltd a/c			
3 Oct.	Cheque	3,400	1 Oct.	Balance b/d	3,400
			20 Oct.	Purchases	658
31 Oct.	Balance c/d	893	25 Oct.	Purchases	235
		4,293			4,293
			1 Nov.	Balance b/d	893

Figure 8.5 A closed off ledger account

On the credit side of the account you will notice something new – an entry labelled 'balance b/d' (balance brought down). This is the result of a previous closing off of this account. Leave this aside for a moment. To close off an account, first add up the transactions on both sides of the account: in Figure 8.5, the debit total is £3,400, the credit total is £4,293. Next, subtract the smaller total from the larger total: i.e. £4,293 − £3,400 = £893. This amount (£893) is then entered on the smaller side and called 'balance carried down', which usually is shortened to 'balance c/d'. You can see the balance carried down on the debit side of the account of AB Supplies Ltd above. Now, both sides of the account should total the same amount, i.e. £4,293. A line or two below where you enter the balance carried down, total both sides of the account on the same line, as shown. Last, below these totals you enter a 'balance brought down', usually shortened to 'balance b/d'. The balance brought down amount is the same amount as the carried down amount, but is posted on the opposite side – remember every debit must have a credit. You will notice that the date for the balance brought down is the next calendar date, i.e. usually the first day of the next month or year. The process of closing off ledger accounts also explains the balance brought down on 1 October in the account of AB Supplies Ltd above. This balance of £3,400 would have been the balance carried down as at 30 September.

You can also present ledger accounts in a three-column format. This is useful if you use a spreadsheet for your ledger accounts. Figure 8.6 shows the account for AB Supplies Ltd using a three-column format. You can see that the balance is calculated after each entry, so you always have a balance carried down available.

AB Supplies Ltd a/c	Debit	Credit	Balance
1 Oct. Balance b/d		3,400	3,400
3 Oct. Cheque	3,400		0
20 Oct. Purchases		658	658
25 Oct. Purchases		235	893

Figure 8.6 A ledger account in three-column format

The nominal and personal ledgers

You learned about the different types of ledger in Chapters 3 and 4 – the nominal and personal ledgers. The account of AB Supplies Ltd in Figure 8.6, for example, is a personal account. All personal accounts for customers and suppliers are kept in the personal ledger. These ledgers are sometimes called accounts receivable or debtors ledger for customers and accounts payable or creditors ledger for suppliers. In the personal ledgers, all transactions – purchases, sales, receipts and payments, etc. – are entered into each personal account from the day books. Therefore it is possible to track how much each customer owes and, similarly, how much is owed to each supplier. Accounts receivable and accounts payable, as business functions (departments), are quite often separated in an organisation, one person being responsible for each, and this is the historic reason for having personal ledgers.

The nominal (or general) ledger is used for all 'non-personal' accounts. This ledger is traditionally the realm of accountants, with book-keepers often responsible for the personal ledgers. The nominal ledger will have accounts like a bank account, a sales account, a motor expenses account, etc. Data from the day books is recorded in such accounts, but in summary format. Totals rather than individual entries from the day books are entered in what are often referred to as 'control accounts'. Each personal ledger has a control account in the nominal ledger – the accounts receivable (or debtors) control account and the accounts payable (or creditors) control account.

In Figure 8.7, you can see an example of an accounts payable (or creditors) control account based on day books used in Chapters 4 and 5. Earlier, we had the account of AB Supplies Ltd. The accounts payable control account is very similar, but represents all supplier accounts from the personal ledger used for suppliers.

	Accounts payable control a/c		
(See Figure 5.7) Cheque payments book	7,970	Balance b/d	10,567
		Purchases day book	11,968 (see Figure 4.1)
Balance c/d	14,565		
	22,535		22,535
		Balance b/d	14,565

Figure 8.7 Accounts payable control account

If you look back at Figure 4.1 (p. 50), you'll see the total of the purchases day book is entered on the credit side as this is a liability account. Likewise, the total of the 'creditors' column from the cheque payments book (Figure 5.7, p. 80) is entered on the debit side. The balance b/d is made up for the sake of completeness, while the balance c/d has been calculated as described earlier.

You might be thinking, why two sets of ledger accounts? The answer is two-fold. First, the daily tasks of keeping track of amounts owed by customers and to suppliers can be delegated – normally to a junior accountant or a book-keeper. Accountants don't need detailed information on individual customers and suppliers to prepare financial statements. A summary in the form of control accounts is enough. Second, a segregation of duties is possible whereby no one person is in control of all accounts and ledgers. Segregation of duties in this way is a fraud prevention measure. Of course, in a small business, segregation may not be possible.

The general journal

There is one day book you have not seen so far. It is called the general journal (or journal for short). It is used more often by accountants, but is included here to complete your understanding of how data gets to the ledger accounts. It is a rather simple day book, with columns for date, narrative and debit/credit entries. Figure 8.8 shows an example.

Great Garages

Journal

Date	Account	Debit	Credit
31 Oct.	Bad debts	1,175	
	Debtor's control		1,175
	(Customer Steve Grey bankrupt)		

Figure 8.8 The general journal

The general journal is used to post any transactions that are not posted in any other day book. In the example in Figure 8.8, the entry shows that a customer, Steve Grey (look back at the sales day book in Figure 3.3 on p. 35), has gone bankrupt and we now will not be paid. When this happens, an expense called a 'bad debt' occurs. As this bad debt is an expense and is being increased, the account is debited, hence the entry under the debit column. The amount owed by this customer and the total amount owed (i.e. assets) would be reduced, hence the entry under the credit column.

The general journal would also be used to post entries like depreciation, the value of closing stock (see Chapter 9) or perhaps adjustments made by accountants. The most important thing is to write a narrative of some kind, otherwise it can be hard for someone else to follow your work.

The trial balance

If the rules of double-entry accounting are applied correctly, the total of debits on all accounts should equal the total credits. As ledger entries form the basis of financial statements, they need to be correct. To check if the ledger accounts do comply with the rules of double-entry, something called a trial balance is prepared.

A trial balance takes all account balances in the nominal ledger (i.e. the balances b/d) and lists them in two columns according to whether they are debit or credit balances. Figure 8.9 shows an example which uses the data from the day books of Great Garages in Chapters 3, 4 and 5 (Figures 3.3, 4.1, 4.5, 5.1, 5.13 and the general journal in Figure 8.8 above), and I have completed the ledger accounts and calculated the closing balances. You will notice that there is an opening balance b/d on the bank account, VAT account and petty cash account and also a capital account (which is explained in more detail in Chapter 9).

Debtors control account			
Sales	9,784.50	Cash receipts	6,250.00
		Journal – bad debt	1,175.00
		Balance c/d	2,359.50
	9,784.50		9,784.50
Balance b/d	2,359.50		

Creditors control account			
Bank	7,970.00	Purchases	11,968.00
Balance c/d	3,998.00		
	11,968.00		11,968.00
		Balance b/d	3,998.00

Bank account			
Balance b/d	5,437.00	Cheques	26,835.00
Debtors	6,250.00		
Utilities refund	10.00		
Cash sales	240.00		
Balance c/d	14,898.00		
	21,398.00		26,835.00
		Balance b/d	14,898.00

Bad debts account			
Debtors	1,175.00	Balance c/d	1,175.00
Balance b/d	1,175.00		

Sales account			
Balance c/d	8,640.00	Debtors	8,440.00
		Cash sales	200.00
	8,640.00		8,640.00
		Balance b/d	8,640.00

Figure 8.9 Ledger accounts and trial balance of Great Garages

Purchases account			
Creditors	10,260.00	Balance c/d	10,260.00
Balance b/d	10,260.00		

VAT account			
Creditors	1,708.00	Balance b/d	3,000.00
Bank	3,000.00	Debtors	1,344.50
		Cash sales	40.00
		Balance c/d	323.50
	4,708.00		1,708.00
Balance b/d	323.50		

Utilities account			
Bank	130.00	Cash receipts	10.00
		Balance c/d	120.00
	130.00		130.00
Balance b/d	120.00		

Wages account			
Bank	500.00	Balance c/d	500.00
Balance b/d	500.00		

Telephone account			
Bank	210.00	Balance c/d	210.00
Balance b/d	210.00		

Vans account			
Bank	15,000.00	Balance c/d	15,000.00
Balance b/d	15,000.00		

Petty cash account			
Balance b/d	100.00	Misc Expenses	10.09
Bank	10.00	Balance c/d	99.91
	110.00		110.00
Balance b/d	99.91		

Bank charges account			
Bank	15.00	Balance c/d	15.00
Balance b/d	15.00		

Miscellaneous expenses			
Petty cash	10.09	Balance c/d	10.09
Balance b/d	10.09		

Capital a/c			
		Balance b/d	2,537.00

Figure 8.9 continued

Trial balance of Great Garages as at 31 October

	Debit £	Credit £
Debtors	2,359.50	
Creditors		3,998.00
Bank		14,898.00
Bad debts	1,175.00	
Sales		8,640.00
Purchases	10,260.00	
VAT	323.50	
Utilities	120.00	
Wages	500.00	
Telephone	210.00	
Vans	15,000.00	
Petty cash	99.91	
Miscellaneous expenses	10.09	
Bank charges	15.00	
Capital		2,537.00
	30,073.00	30,073.00

Figure 8.9 continued

I have then taken the balances brought down (balance b/d) from each nominal ledger account and simply placed them in the respective column of the trial balance. For example, the debtors balance b/d is £2,359.50 debit, so this goes in the debit column. The debit and credit totals in the trial balance are equal, proving that the principles of the double-entry system have been applied correctly in the ledger accounts.

 **brilliant** tip

If a trial balance does not balance, don't leave it. Do try to find the mistake.

You might have noticed that the columns in the trial balance follow a pattern. The debit column contains balances of either asset or expense accounts, whereas the credit column contains balances of liability, income or capital accounts (which are explained in Chapter 9). For example, the purchases figure is an expense as shown in the debit column in Figure 8.9, sales is an income and is in the credit column, and the bank balance is overdrawn (liability) and is in the credit column.

If a trial balance balances, does this mean that all figures and ledger accounts are 100 per cent accurate? The answer is no, for a number of reasons as follows:

- Transactions may have been omitted completely from the day books and thus were never recorded in the ledgers. For example, a supplier's invoice may have been misplaced or not received, and thus not entered anywhere. This type of error is referred to as an error of omission.

- A correct entry may have been made to a wrong account. For example, a sale to a credit customer, A. Baker, was posted to the debit side of the ledger account for A. Barker. The sale was correctly credited to the sales account. The debits and credits will be equal, but incorrect as A. Barker's account shows a sale not made to him. This type of error is referred to as an error of commission.

- A ledger entry could be reversed. For example, you post a credit sale to the credit side of a debtor's account and the debit side of the sales account. This would of course be wrong, but the trial balance would be OK as the double-entry principles have been followed.

- Two errors might compensate each other. For example, you may have over-added both the purchases and sales account by £1,000. As the purchases normally would have a debit balance, and sales a credit balance, one error cancels the other.

- An entry could have been taken incorrectly from the day books. For example, the total sales in the sales day book might read £18,000, but you mis-read this as £13,000 and entered it in the sales and debtors accounts as £13,000. This type of error is referred to as an error of original entry.

- Finally, an entry could be made to the wrong class of account. For example, the purchase of a delivery van could be debited to a motor expenses account (expense) and not to a motor vans account (asset). This type of error is called an error of principle. Again, the principles of double entry have been applied, so the trial balance would not reveal such an error.

Locating and preventing errors

Having explained the kinds of mistakes that might not be revealed by a trial balance, let's see how to begin to locate errors in the ledgers and then look at some simple procedures to prevent errors.

The trial balance is incorrect

If the trial balance does not balance, you have made a mistake somewhere in your ledger entries or in the trial balance preparation. There are a number of things you can do to find the mistake. These could include the following:

● Re-check the totals of each column of the trial balance to make sure your addition is correct.

● Make sure the balances from each ledger account are in the correct column of the trial balance.

● Make sure you have transcribed all balances correctly from the ledger accounts to the trial balance.

● If the difference on the trial balance is divisible evenly by nine, you have transposed figures somewhere. For example, you have used £910 in one place and £901 in another. This can help you to find differences a little more quickly.

If these steps do not help, you will have to check each ledger account to ensure your adding/subtracting is correct.

Error prevention

Following, you'll see some examples of the ledger accounts and trial balance in QuickBooks. One major advantage of accounting software is that you cannot but apply the rules of double entry. If you post any transaction with unequal debits and credits, you'll get an error message from the software and will be prevented from continuing until the debits and credits are equal.

There are a number of other ways to limit any potential errors in ledger accounts. These measures will not prevent all errors and/or omissions, but are likely to capture the vast majority of mistakes.

- Do a bank reconciliation regularly – as shown in Chapter 5. A bank reconciliation can pick up mistakes and omissions in the day books.

- Check the balances between the personal ledgers and nominal ledger control accounts. Remember that the personal ledgers record all individual transactions of customers and suppliers from the day book, whereas the control accounts are a summary of these balances using the totals from the day books. The balance on the control accounts (for customers and suppliers) should be the same as the total of all balances on the respective personal ledger. If not, there are errors somewhere. This kind of check at least points to the fact that an error exists. You'll then have to find reasons for the difference. It could be posting errors, totting errors, etc. A good place to start is to ensure that all entries in the control accounts are actually in the personal accounts. For example, the accountant might enter a bad debt in the debtors control account and not inform the book-keeper to enter it on the customer's account in the personal ledger.

- Do a creditors reconciliation. This process is similar to a bank reconciliation. Your suppliers will send you a statement of account usually each month. You can use this statement to compare against the balance in your personal ledger. You might find, for example, that a supplier's invoice is missing. This kind of check can prevent errors of omission, for example.

The trial balance and financial statements

A trial balance has another important function and that is to help in the preparation of financial statements, i.e. the income statement and balance sheet. If you look at the trial balance in Figure 8.9, you'll see it is at a month-end. Although a trial balance can be prepared at any time, it is more often prepared at a month- or year-end to help prepare the financial statements. It is very useful for this purpose as it is a summary of all accounts from which we can pick 1. the income and expenses for the income statement, and 2. assets, liabilities and capital for the balance sheet. Chapter 9 gives more details on how the financial statements are prepared.

Port Meadow Locksmiths Ltd
General Ledger
As at 31 December 2008

Type	Date	Num.	Name	Memo	Split	Amount	Balance
Current Account							8,880.78
Cheque	10/12/2008	SO	Thames Council		-SPLIT-	-111.00	8,769.78
Cheque	15/12/2008	DD	National Bank	quarterly loan r...	-SPLIT-	-209.25	8,560.53
Cheque	31/12/2008	100027	National Access		-SPLIT-	-130.00	8,430.53
Bill Pmt -Cheque	31/12/2008	12345	City Safe Wholesale		Accounts Payable	-5,750.74	2,679.79
Payment	31/12/2008		Prestige Estates:GS Pr...		Accounts Recei...	1,437.41	4,117.20
Bill Pmt -Cheque	31/12/2008	500134	Stuart Leven		Accounts Payable	-3,000.00	1,117.20
Cheque	31/12/2008	500135	Martin Quinn		Professional Fees	-200.00	917.20
Total Current Account						-7,963.58	917.20

Figure 8.10 A ledger account in QuickBooks

Ledger accounts and the trial balance in QuickBooks

Ledger accounts

In Chapters 3, 4 and 5, you've seen how software like QuickBooks does a lot of the ledger accounts' work once a business transaction (invoice, cheque, cash receipt, etc.) is entered. Let's look at ledger accounts in QuickBooks. Figure 8.10 shows a ledger account in QuickBooks, in this example the ledger account for a bank current account.

This looks a little like the three-column ledger account shown in Figure 8.6. The words debit and credit are not used very often in QuickBooks. Here, in the bank current account, a negative number means credit, a positive means debit. The balance is shown in the right-most column after each transaction. You can also see a narrative for each transaction, referring to the customer or supplier name, for example.

Trial balance

In the ledger account from QuickBooks shown in Figure 8.10, the balance on the account is recalculated constantly after each transaction. Closing off accounts therefore is not needed. This means you can run a trial balance at any time. Figure 8.11 shows an example of a trial balance from QuickBooks.

It looks just like a trial balance prepared manually. There are a lot of accounts listed in this example, but remember it is prepared automatically as each and every business transaction is entered in the software. Therefore, the work is minimal compared with manually preparing a trial balance. And remember too that the trial balance will always balance as accounting software will always ensure double-entry principles are applied.

		2:51 PM	**Port Meadow Locksmiths Ltd**	

2:51 PM   **Port Meadow Locksmiths Ltd**
31/12/08   **Trial Balance**
Accrual Basis   **As at 30 November 2008**

	30 Nov 08	
	Debit	Credit
Current Account	8,880.78	
Cash Account	49.55	
Accounts Receivable	14,989.82	
Stock	1,287.44	
Undeposited Funds	4,118.68	
Plant & Equipment:Cost Plant & Equip	850.00	
Computer equipment:Cost Computer E...	600.00	
Vehicles:Cost Vehicles	3,750.00	
Accounts Payable		20,158.58
Credit Card Account		1,994.96
Bank Loan		2,700.00
Director's Loan		3,500.00
Payroll Liabilities		349.67
VAT Liability		528.67
Share Capital		1,000.00
Retained Earnings		795.00
Sales		35,930.04
Locks and Safes Purchases	19,334.48	
Advertising	500.00	
Bank Service Charges	11.70	
Dues and Subscriptions	12.50	
Insurance	227.83	
Interest Expense	118.50	
Motor Expense	138.77	
Office Supplies	251.47	
Payroll Expenses	5,996.84	
Rent & Rates	6,555.00	
Software Expense	34.03	
Telephone	246.97	
Utilities	214.00	
Interest Received		16.44
Subletting Income		1,695.00
Dividends	500.00	
TOTAL	**68,668.36**	**68,668.36**

Figure 8.11 A trial balance report from QuickBooks

brilliant recap

- The double-entry system sets the rules for entering business transactions in a ledger account.

- The personal ledgers hold accounts of suppliers and customers, with the nominal ledger having impersonal accounts.

- At month- or year-end, ledger accounts are closed off, with the balances b/d used to prepare a trial balance.

- The trial balance has two purposes: 1. to check that double-entry rules have been applied correctly and 2. to help prepare financial statements (see Chapter 9).

- Accounting software like QuickBooks updates ledger accounts and the trial balance as each business transaction is entered. This saves a lot of effort for the book-keeper and accountants.

CHAPTER 9

An introduction to financial statements

W e're now ready to see how two important financial statements, the income statement and the balance sheet, are prepared. The income statement is also known as the profit and loss account. The latter term is used more commonly for small businesses. The term 'income statement' is required by European Union law (since 2004) to be used for public companies and many private companies also use it.

In this chapter you'll learn how to 1. use the trial balance to prepare financial statements and 2. introduce some adjustments/additions which normally are required to be made to the trial balance before 'final' financial statements are available. To keep things simple, this chapter assumes the business is a sole trader. Financial statements of limited companies are a little more complex and we'll see those towards the end of the chapter.

The income statement

The income statement shows the profit or loss of a business for a period of time, usually a month or year. It shows the income and expenses of a business. In other words, it depicts the financial performance of a business. If you are a sole trader, the income statement does not have to conform to any particular layout. However, accounting standards (rules followed by accountants), which dictate the layout of financial statements for companies, are often followed by accountants for other business forms. Therefore, the layout of the income statement is quite similar regardless of the business type.

The trial balance of Great Garages from Chapter 8 is shown again in Figure 9.1. Let's use this to prepare an income statement. This is quite an easy task; we just use the trial balance to identify the income and expenses of the business. Some notes are added to the right of the trial balance to show if the account is an asset, liability, income, etc.

Trial balance of Great Garages as at 31 October

	Debit £	Credit £	*Account type*
Debtors	2,359.50		*Asset*
Creditors		3,998.00	*Liability*
Bank		14,898.00	*Liability*
Bad debts	1,175.00		*Expense*
Sales		8,640.00	*Income*
Purchases	10,260.00		*Expense*
VAT	323.50		*Asset*
Utilities	120.00		*Expense*
Wages	500.00		*Expense*
Telephone	210.00		*Expense*
Vans	15,000.00		*Asset*
Petty cash	99.91		*Asset*
Miscellaneous expenses	10.09		*Expense*
Bank charges	15.00		*Expense*
Capital		2,537.00	*Capital*
	30,073.00	30,073.00	

Figure 9.1 Trial balance of Great Garages

brilliant tip

The word income in an income statement means income from operations, i.e. income generated from what your business does. This normally means sales income. Other income, such as bank interest, will be identified separately in an income statement.

Looking at each item on the trial balance, the only income account is sales. The expenses are bad debts, purchases, utilities, wages, telephone, miscellaneous expenses and bank charges. This is all we need to prepare the income statement. Before we do, here is a sample income statement.

Income statement of XYZ for the year ended 31 December 200X

	£	£
Sales		20,000
Cost of sales		(14,000)
Gross profit		7,000
Light and heat	1,500	
Motor expenses	2,000	
Insurance	1,600	
Wages	1,400	
		6,500
Operating profit		1,500

There are some new terms, which you'll need to know.

 brilliant definitions

Cost of sales is a figure closely related to the sales figure. The cost of a sale may be identified as a product is made. For example, in a custom engineering business, costs may be accumulated for each order. More often, cost of sales is calculated only when an income statement is required. For now, think of cost of sales as the purchase price of goods you sell. Additional costs, like transport or customs duties, are also included in cost of sales.

Gross profit is sales less cost of sales. This is simply the profit from trading, before deducting expenses. Gross profit less expenses is the operating (net) profit.

Operating profit is the amount of money generated by the normal trading activities of a business. As mentioned earlier, a business may have other sources of income, such as bank interest, which could now be added to this figure.

Now back to Great Garages. Taking the income and expenses from the trial balance in Figure 9.1, the income statement for the month of October would look like that shown in Figure 9.2.

Income statement of Great Garages
for the month ended 31 October 2009

	£	£
Sales		8,640
Cost of sales		(10,260)
Gross profit		(1,620)
Bad debts	1,175	
Utilities	120	
Wages	500	
Telephone	210	
Miscellaneous expenses	10	
Bank charges	15	
		2,030
Operating loss		(3,650)

Figure 9.2 Income statement of Great Garages

You might notice that the heading of the income statement says 'for the month ended October'. This makes sense, as to compare incomes and expenses over a time period means you can calculate a profit or loss for that time period. The headings of financial statements take the form 'who', 'what' and 'when', i.e. who is the business, what financial statement it is, when it is for.

> the income statement simply lists income, expenditure and profits/losses

That's it for the income statement. No matter how simple or complex a business, the income statement simply lists income, expenditure and profits/losses. Now let's see what making a profit means for your business.

The effect of profit on capital

In Figure 9.2 the income statement of Great Garages showed a loss of £3,650. What does this mean for the business owner? It means the value of the capital of the business has decreased by £3,650.

Do you recall the accounting equation from Chapter 1? It stated assets minus liabilities equals capital. Look back at Figure 9.1 and you'll see a capital account with a credit balance of £2,537. This figure was calculated previously in Chapter 8 (see Figure 8.9, p. 153) as the difference between assets and liabilities, i.e. the opening balances on the bank account of £5,437 + petty cash account £100 – VAT account £3,000. Thus, the capital at the start of October for Great Garages was £2,537. Any profit or loss made is reflected in the capital account too, so the capital of Great Garages will now be (£1,113) i.e. £2,537−£3,650. Yes, it is possible to have a negative capital, but not for too long as ultimately this means a business is running at a loss. The following example provides a further illustration of the relationship between profits and capital.

 **example**

Tom's business has goods in stock valued at £3,000. He bought these goods on credit, so has a liability. Putting these figures into the accounting equation, the capital would be nil. Suppose he sells the goods for £5,000, thus making a profit of £2,000. The stock value is now nil and, assuming the monies from the sale are lodged to the bank account, the bank balance is £5,000. Now, putting the figures into the accounting equation, we get:

Assets	Liabilities	Capital
Bank, £5,000	Creditors, £3,000	£2,000

You can see the capital has increased by the amount of profit made.

You might be thinking, how can the business owner obtain some of the profits for themselves? If a sole trader makes a profit, they usually withdraw some of the profits to cover personal living expenses. Any such amounts are called drawings. Drawings are not the same as wages, since wages relate to employees and you can't employ yourself. Drawings are in fact a reduction in the capital of the business and most sole traders take some form of cash drawing on a regular basis. Of course, a sole trader will have to pay tax on profits and this is also a reduction in the capital of the business.

From this example, you might have guessed by now that the profits/losses from the income statement are a link between it and the balance sheet, so let's look at a balance sheet.

The balance sheet

A balance sheet is a list of the assets, liabilities and capital of a business at any point in time. Often it is referred to as a statement of the financial position of a business, as it shows what the business has (assets), what it owes (liabilities) and how it is financed (capital). You already know what assets, liabilities and capital are from Chapter 1, so let's see how they appear in the balance sheet. As suggested by the name 'balance sheet', something must balance. The balance sheet is actually a representation of the accounting equation, so by definition the balance sheet will balance. Or look at it another way:

1 You start off with a trial balance that balances.

2 You take all income and expenses in the trial balance to the income statement and work out a profit or loss.

3 You take the profit to the balance sheet with all remaining items from the trial balance.

4 Thus, the balance sheet would have to balance.

Before you see a balance sheet, let's see how assets and liabilities normally are grouped for the purposes of the balance sheet. Refer back to Chapter 1 if you're unsure of the nature of assets and liabilities.

Current assets

These are assets that are short-term in nature. Current assets normally meet one of the following characteristics:

● They are held for use or resale by the business as part of normal day-to-day operations.

● They are expected to be sold within one year.

● They are held primarily for trading purposes.

● They are cash, or equivalent to cash (i.e. can be sold for cash quickly).

The most common current assets are inventories (stocks), amounts owed by customers (trade receivables/debtors) and cash/cash in the bank. The level of each held by a business depends on the nature of the business. For example, a service business is not likely to have any stocks.

Non-current assets

As noted in Chapter 7, non-current (or fixed) assets are assets that are not current assets. They are held by a business for the long term and usually have a productive use. Examples would be premises, vans and office furniture. What is classified as a non-current asset depends too on the nature of the business. For example, a car may be a non-current asset of your business, but would be a current asset (i.e. inventory) of a car manufacturer.

Current liabilities

Current liabilities are amounts owed that are due to be paid within one year. To be a little more precise, they normally meet one of the following criteria:

- They are paid within the normal course of business.
- They are due to be paid within one year of the balance sheet date.
- They are held for trading purposes.
- There is no right to extend the settlement period beyond one year.

Examples of current liabilities are amounts owing to suppliers (trade payables/creditors), amounts owing to tax authorities and a bank overdraft.

Non-current liabilities

Non-current liabilities are liabilities other than current liabilities. Typical examples are long-term bank loans. Quite often, a balance sheet will show bank loans split into the portion due within one year, which is shown as a current liability, and the portion due after one year, shown as a non-current liability.

Layout of the balance sheet

A balance sheet normally is presented in a vertical layout, as shown in Figure 9.3. This layout shows assets grouped on the top portion of the balance sheet, and capital and liabilities on the bottom portion.

As you can see, the total of the assets is equal to the total of liabilities plus capital, so the balance sheet balances. You may see balance sheets presented differently, but it will always have two totals that equal each other.

Balance sheet of XYZ as at 31 December 2009

Non-current assets		£
Property		55
Plant & equipment		67
Motor van		24
		146
Current assets		
Inventories	23	
Trade receivables	23	
Cash at bank	59	
		105
		251
Capital		
Owners capital		100
Non-current liabilities		
Long-term bank loan		65
Current liabilities		
Trade payables	56	
Taxation owing	30	86
		251

Figure 9.3 Sample balance sheet

For example, Figure 9.3 could be presented with assets and liabilities (as a deduction) on the upper portion, and capital in the lower portion.

Let's return to the Great Garages example. From the trial balance and income statement in Figures 9.1 and 9.2, the balance sheet would be as shown in Figure 9.4.

The capital figure shown in the balance sheet is as calculated earlier, i.e. (£1,113). You can see that the two sets of totals agree, so the balance sheet balances.

That's it for the balance sheet. Now that you know the basics of both the income statement and the balance sheet, let's look at some more items that need to be examined when these statements are being prepared.

Balance sheet of Great Garages as at 31 December 2009

Non-current assets		£
Motor van		15,000
		15,000
Current assets		
Debtors	2,360	
Petty cash	100	
VAT	323	
		2,783
		17,783
Capital		
Owners capital		(1,113)
Current liabilities		
Creditors	3,998	
Bank overdraft	14,898	
		18,896
		17,783

Figure 9.4 Balance sheet of Great Garages

Preparing the financial statements

A trial balance is not the only thing needed when an income statement and balance sheet are to be prepared. Even if you are pretty good at keeping your day books and ledgers (either manually or using software), there will be some additional work. Typically, you'll have a process that would be something like this:

1 Get a trial balance to ensure it balances.

2 Check the trial balance for any odd looking figures (maybe a balance looks too large). If so, check to see if errors were made in the day books or ledgers. Correct any errors and get a new trial balance.

3 Provide for/adjust expenses so that all expenses relate only to the period of the income statement.

4 Do an inventory count and put a value on it.

5 Calculate depreciation on non-current assets.

6 Prepare the income statement and balance sheet.

Businesses that keep manual records often leave all these steps to their accountant. If you use software, steps 4 and 5 may happen automatically. Accountants often refer to the above steps as 'period-end adjustments'. Chapter 7 has already detailed inventory and depreciation, but we'll see now how the figures are used in the financial statements. All of the adjustments mentioned would be done most likely by an accountant and recorded in the general journal.

Accruals and prepayments

The accruals concept was introduced in Chapter 1. To refresh your memory, it means that income and expenditure are accounted for when a transaction occurs, not when cash is paid. It is often called the 'matching' concept, too, as it means revenues and costs should be matched against each other when a transaction occurs.

In practical terms this means that when financial statements are prepared, bills for expenses within the accounting period only (i.e. the period of the income statement) need to be included. It is highly unlikely that all bills will have been received when the income statement is being prepared and thus some need to be 'accrued' for. Likewise, some expenses may have been paid during an accounting period, but relate to a later period. Such 'prepayments' need to be removed. Consider the following example:

Fred's accounting year ends on 30 June. He is preparing his income statement. He discovers he has not yet received a mobile phone bill for June. His normal monthly bill is £80. He is also missing a bill for electricity for the month of June, which he estimates would be £50. Fred rents his office for £10,000 per annum and pays this up-front on 1 January each year.

What are the accruals and prepayments in this example? Jot your answer in the space below.

_____

_____

_____

The mobile phone bill and the electricity bill need to be accrued as they are costs within Fred's accounting year and should be matched against his income for the same period in the income statement. It does not matter if his estimates are not 100 per cent accurate. Half of the rent (January to June) relates to Fred's income statement for this year, half to next year. Items like these are recorded in the general journal, as shown in Figure 9.5.

Fred's business

General journal	Debit £	Credit £
Telephone	80	
Accrued expenses		80
(Telephone bill for June accrued)		
Light & heat	50	
Accrued expenses		50
(Telephone bill for June accrued)		
Rent		5,000
Prepaid expenses	5,000	
(Rent paid in advance on 1 Jan.)		

Figure 9.5 Accruals and prepayments of Fred's business

You can see the telephone and light & heat accounts are being debited, or increased. This is what you would expect as the bills not yet received would increase the expense for the year. The expenses in the income statement would also increase as a result. An account called 'accrued expenses' is being credited in both cases. This is a liability, or more correctly a current liability, in the balance sheet. The rent account is being credited, reducing the expense as the prepaid portion of the rent does not relate to this year. The corresponding debit is to a 'prepaid expenses' account, which is treated as a current asset in the balance sheet.

Accruals and prepayments affect both the income statement and the balance sheet. Accruals in particular may be estimates of expenses for which bills have not yet been received. For this reason, accountants and tax inspectors keep a close eye on accruals in particular, as it is easy to 'stick in an accrual' to reduce profits! This aside, accruals and prepayments need to be addressed when preparing the financial statements as not to do so will give an inaccurate picture of the true profit of the business for an accounting period.

Stock valuation

Chapter 7 detailed a number of tasks and roles of the book-keeper in relation to stocks. Here we'll see how the value of stocks affects the financial statements. If a business buys and sells goods, it is likely to have stocks at the end of an accounting year. This stock was purchased during the year, with invoices recorded as a purchase in the purchases day book (or in your accounting software). Do you think stock held at the end of a year is a cost for the current accounting year or the next? Write what you think in the space provided.

_____

_____

_____

_____

This is another case of the accruals concept in action, as the cost of the goods will not be expensed (or matched) against a sale until the following year at least.

Once a value has been placed on stock at the year-end, it is used to reduce the cost of sales figure in the income statement. Our earlier notion of cost of sales in the income statement can be modified to:

Opening stock + purchases − closing stock

Stock is also an asset, more correctly a current asset. The value of stock at the end of the accounting period thus is entered in the balance sheet under current assets. The value of stock is important since it affects gross profit. A higher closing stock value will lower the cost of sales. A lower cost of sales, in turn, means a higher gross profit. Not bad, you might think, but higher profits mean higher taxes. Or, if you were cynical, you might think a business could build up stock deliberately to inflate profits! Let's just say that if your business had a manager who was paid a bonus on profits, increasing stock might increase the bonus.

higher profits mean higher taxes

Look back at Figures 9.2 and 9.4, the financial statements of Great Garages. Suppose the value of stock at the end of October was £6,000. This would reduce the cost of sales and add an asset to the balance sheet. Figure 9.6 shows a new set of financial statements of the business.

**Income statement of Great Garages
for the month ended 31 October 2009**

	£	£
Sales		8,640
Cost of sales		(4,260)
Gross profit		4,380
Bad debts	1,175	
Utilities	120	
Wages	500	
Telephone	210	
Miscellaneous expenses	10	
Bank charges	15	
		2,030
Operating profit		2,350

Balance sheet of Great Garages as at 31 October 2009

Non-current assets	£	
Motor van		15,000
		15,000
Current assets		
Inventories	6,000	
Debtors	2,360	
Petty cash	100	
VAT	323	
		8,783
		23,783
Capital		
Owners capital		4,887
Current liabilities		
Creditors	3,998	
Bank overdraft	14,898	
		18,896
		23,783

Figure 9.6 Financial statements of Great Garages

The income statement is now showing a profit of £2,350, we have an asset for stock on the balance sheet (£6,000) and the capital account balance has been adjusted accordingly (£2,537 + £2,350 = £ 4,887).

Depreciation

Chapter 7 showed you how to estimate the depreciation charge. The charge for each year is an expense in the income statement. It is also shown in the balance sheet as accumulated depreciation, which is the sum of depreciation charges for all previous years. For example, let's assume an asset has a cost of £5,000 and is depreciated using the straight-line method over 5 years, i.e. £1,000 per annum. The income statement will show the expense each year at £1,000, and the balance sheet will show the asset as follows:

	Year 1	Year 2	Year 3	Year 4	Year 5
Cost	£5,000	£5,000	£5,000	£5,000	£5,000
Accumulated depreciation	£1,000	£2,000	£3,000	£4,000	£5,000
Book value	£4,000	£3,000	£2,000	£1,000	£Nil

If you want to think about depreciation in double-entry terms, each year the depreciation expense account will be debited and the accumulated depreciation account is credited. At year-end, the depreciation will be calculated, probably by the accountants, and entered in the ledgers and financial statements.

Bad debts

A bad debt occurs when a customer cannot pay a debt owing. The bad debt is shown in the income statement as an expense and the amount owing by debtors will be reduced in the balance. This entry would be recorded in the journal as the bad debts occur, and not just at year-end.

However, most businesses will have what is called a 'provision for bad debts'. This provision tries to estimate the likely amount of bad debts from the turnover of a business. This is in fact another application of the accruals concept, as the estimated bad debts that may occur in the future are accounted for in the current year accounts. The following example shows the effects on the financial statements.

 **example**

The debtors of a business at the end of the accounting years 2009 and 2008 were £300,000 and £240,000 respectively. Past experience shows that approximately 1% of debts turn bad. Based on this information, a provision for bad debts would be calculated at £3,000 in 2008. This amount would appear in the income statement as an expense and would be deducted from debtors in the balance sheet. In ledger accounts, this would be represented as:

| Debit | Bad debt expense a/c | £3,000 |
| Credit | Provision for bad debts | £3,000 |

In 2009, the provision would be 1% of £200,000, which is £2,000. Something different happens this time – only the increase or decrease in the provision is included in the income statement. So in this example, £1,000 would be shown in the income statement as a deduction from expenses, with the provision in the balance sheet reduced to £2,000. In ledger accounts, this would be represented as:

| Credit | Bad debt expense a/c | £1,000 (reducing the expense) |
| Debit | Provision for bad debts | £1,000 (balance sheet) |

You can now see that an initial trial balance is the starting point in preparing the income statement and the balance sheet. Expenses are examined to see if accruals or prepayments apply, a closing stock value is obtained and included, depreciation on non-current assets is calculated and provisions may be calculated and/or adjusted. If, as book-keeper, you can do all this, you will have quite accurate financial statements. If you can't, it does not mean that your financial statements are not good enough to help you make business decisions, it just means the accountant has some work to do.

A final point on the income statement

It may appear obvious, but the income statement, or profit and loss account as it's more traditionally called, is actually part of the double-entry system. Earlier in Figure 9.1, the trial balance showed the items that appear on the income statement. After a trial balance is prepared, according to the principles of double-entry accounting, these accounts (i.e. the income and expense accounts) would be closed off to the profit and loss account. For example, the sales account would not have a balance brought down on the credit side of £8,640. Instead, the sales account would be debited with the amount of £8,640 and the profit and loss account credited with the same amount. Likewise other income and expense accounts would be closed off to the profit and loss account. The balance on the profit and loss account, which would be the profit or loss, is then transferred to the capital account. Are you confused yet? In practice, it's easy to appreciate why the income statement is not shown as a ledger account. If it were, the informational value of it might be lost – remember that one purpose of accounting is to communicate information. Therefore, it is highly unlikely you will ever see an income statement in any other format than a vertical columnar format.

> one purpose of accounting is to communicate information

Financial statements in QuickBooks

In earlier chapters you saw how accounting software like QuickBooks automatically compiles financial statements as business transactions are entered. Let's look at some of the financial statement reports that QuickBooks can generate. First, Figure 9.7 shows an example of an income statement from a sample company in QuickBooks.

The layout, while containing more expenses than the earlier examples, is pretty much the same. Only one year is shown in this example. You can select any time period (year, month, quarter or custom dates) and also place comparatives from previous years or months. Remember, such reports can be run at any time and there is no need to wait until month-end or year-end.

Port Meadow Locksmiths
Income Statement
January through December 2008

	Jan - Dec 08
Ordinary income/expense	
Income	
Sales	37,102.35
Total income	37,102.35
Cost of goods sold	
Locks and safes purchases	19,609.24
Total COGS	19,609.24
Gross profit	17,493.11
Expense	
Advertising	674.47
Bank service charges	11.70
Dues and subscriptions	12.50
Insurance	227.83
Interest expense	177.75
Motor expense	177.49
Office supplies	251.47
Payroll expenses	5,996.84
Professional fees	200.00
Rent & rates	7,666.00
Software expense	34.03
Telephone	246.97
Utilities	1,214.00
Total expense	16,891.05
Net ordinary income	602.06
Other income/expense	
Other income	
Interest received	16.44
Subletting income	1,695.00
Total other income	1,711.44
Net other income	1,711.44
Profit for the Year	**2,313.50**

Figure 9.7 An income statement from QuickBooks

Likewise, a balance sheet can be printed like the one shown in Figure 9.8.

8:33 PM
31/12/08
Accrual Basis

Port Meadow Locksmiths
Balance Sheet - Standard
As at 31 December 2008

	31 Dec 08
ASSETS	
Fixed assets	
Plant & equipment	
Cost plant & equip	850.00
Total plant & equipment	850.00
Computer equipment	
Cost computer equip	600.00
Total computer equipment	600.00
Vehicles	
Cost vehicles	3,750.00
Total vehicles	3,750.00
Total fixed assets	5,200.00
Current assets	
Other current assets	
Stock	1,287.44
Total other current assets	1,287.44
Accounts receivable	
Accounts receivable	13,552.41
Total accounts receivable	13,552.41
Cash at bank and in hand	
Undeposited funds	4,118.68
Current account	1,417.20
Cash account	49.55
Total cash at bank and in hand	5,585.43
Total current assets	20,425.28
Current liabilities	
Accounts payable	
Accounts payable	13,582.84
Total accounts payable	13,582.84
Credit cards	
Credit card account	1,994.96
Total credit cards	1,994.96
Other current liabilities	
Bank loan	2,550.00
Director's loan	3,500.00
Payroll liabilities	349.67
VAT liability	334.31
Total other current liabilities	6,733.98
Total current liabilities	22,311.78
NET CURRENT ASSETS	-1,886.50
TOTAL ASSETS LESS CURRENT LIABILITIES	3,313.50
NET ASSETS	**3,313.50**
Capital and reserves	
Share capital	1,000.00
Retained earnings	795.00
Profit for the year	1,518.50
Shareholder funds	**3,313.50**

Figure 9.8 A balance sheet from QuickBooks

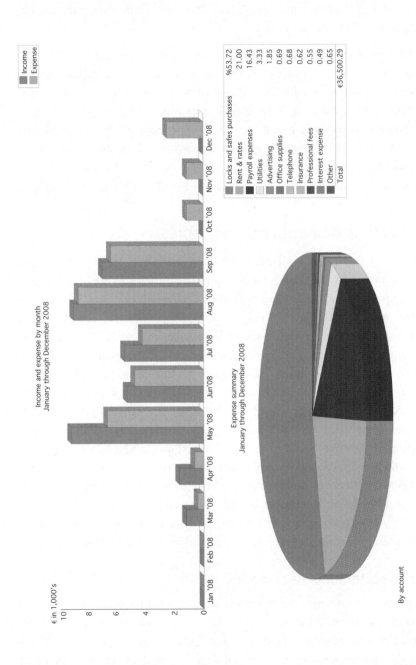

Figure 9.9 An income and expense graph from QuickBooks

This balance sheet shows the assets and liabilities in the upper portion, with capital in the lower portion. Again, this report can be printed for any time period, with comparatives.

In addition to standard reports like those in the preceding figures, most accounting software provides some form of graphical representation of profits, incomes or expenses. These provide a useful snapshot of the business in a very user-friendly way. For example, QuickBooks provides an income and expense graph by month (see Figure 9.9). This offers a quick way to see if a business is making a profit or loss and a breakdown of expenses by type. Many people I know who are not very accounting literate use this method each month to see how their business is doing.

Financial statements of companies

Throughout this chapter all examples used are based on the assumption that a business is a sole trader. Of course many businesses are limited companies, and as companies they are subject to many laws and accounting regulations. Company law actually dictates the format and content of the income statement and balance sheet. Furthermore, public companies are subject to accounting regulations (called accounting standards), which require much more detailed information. Under company law, all companies must publish their financial statements. The detail to be published depends on the size (as detailed by law) of the company. As a book-keeper it's good to have a basic knowledge of how the financial statements of a company are prepared and to be able to read and understand them. The detail and presentation work can be left to an accountant. The principles of preparing the income statement and balance sheet are the same as for a sole trader, but the layout is a little different, although perhaps easier. Internally, it is likely that a company will prepare income statements and balance sheets which are more detailed than required by any laws or standards.

Income statements of companies

The income statement of a company is not too different from that of a sole trader. Companies are of course often more complex businesses. This means that the income statement (and balance sheet) may have some items that are not seen in the accounts of a sole trader. Let's explain some of these items before looking at an example.

First, directors' salaries and other remuneration will be amongst the expenses. Directors are the people responsible for the day-to-day running of a business. They may or may not be shareholders, i.e. owners of the company. Next, auditors' fees will be a normal expense. Auditors verify (i.e. audit) the financial statements of a company. An audit is required by company law. Sole traders and partnerships normally do not need an audit. Finally, the income statement will also show a taxation charge. Companies pay corporation tax on their profits. This tax is shown as an expense in the income statement. However, as you can see in Figure 9.10, you actually will not see many expenses on the face of the income statement.

For the purposes of illustration, let's use a fictional company called ABC plc, i.e. a public company. The layout of the income statement (and later the balance sheet) is in accordance with accounting standards and company law, which applies to UK public companies. Similar formats are used for private companies. If you look at the income statement of a public company on its website, you may find that the income statement has some slight variations, but it will maintain the basic format of this example.

Income statement of ABC plc for the year ended 31 December 2009

	£m
Revenue	20,992
Cost of sales	(14,715)
Gross profit	6,277
Operating costs	(4,191)
Operating profit	2,086
Finance costs	(416)
Finance revenue	170
Share of associates' profit	64
Profit before tax	1,904
Income tax expense	(466)
Profit for the financial year	1,438

Figure 9.10 Income statement of a company

As you can see, the income statement is very brief. Revenue is simply the revenue generated from the operations of the company; in other words, sales. Cost of sales is the same for a sole trader, as is gross profit. Expenses simply are totalled under the heading of 'operating costs' – there is no requirement for a detailed breakdown of expenses. Finance costs and finance revenues are items such as interest paid and received. The 'income tax expense' amount refers to the taxation payable on the profits of the company.

You are probably thinking, is it that simple? Yes, it is in fact. However, much more information is given in what are called the 'notes on the financial statements'. For example, a breakdown of operating costs might be shown on a note as follows:

	£m
Selling and distribution costs	2,675
Administrative expenses	1,474
Other operating expenses	58
Other operating income	(16)
Total	4,191

Still not too detailed, but that's all that's necessary under accounting standards and company law.

Balance sheet of companies

The balance sheet of a company takes a similar format to that of a sole trader in that it lists the assets, liabilities and capital of a company. As with the income statement, there are a number of items normally found on a company balance sheet that are not found on the balance sheet of a sole trader. Let's look at an example in Figure 9.11.

Balance sheet of ABC plc as at 31 December 2009

	£m
ASSETS	
Non-current assets	
Plant, property and equipment	8,226
Intangible assets	4,804
	13,030
Current assets	
Inventories	2,226
Trade receivables	3,199
Cash and cash equivalents	1,333
	6,758
Total assets	19,788
EQUITY	
Equity share capital	187
Preference shares	1
Share premium	2,420
Retained income	5,412
Total equity	8,020
LIABILITIES	
Non-current liabilities	
Loans and borrowings	7,240
Trade and other payables	547
	7,787
Current liabilities	
Trade and other payables	2,956
Current income tax	244
Loans and borrowings	570
Other liabilities	211
	3,981
Total equity and liabilities	19,788

Figure 9.11 A company balance sheet

As with the income statement in Figure 9.10, the balance sheet is not too detailed. The balance sheet has three major headings: assets, equity and liabilities. Equity in companies is similar to the capital of a sole trader.

 brilliant definition

Equity capital is money invested in a company that is not repaid to investors in the normal course of business. It usually represents the amount of money paid for shares by investors.

I'll explain the equity section of the balance sheet later. First, let's look at the assets and liabilities on the balance sheet.

Assets

The assets on a company balance sheet, like those of a sole trader, are split into non-current and current. One key difference in company balance sheets is that accounting regulations give specific headings to be used. Looking first at the non-current assets, you will see some new terms.

Plant, property and equipment
Accounting standards require a company to show only one figure for all its physical assets, i.e. plant, property and equipment. A note to the accounts is required though, which shows the opening balance for each class of asset, additions, disposals and the depreciation figure.

Intangible assets
Non-current assets are often termed tangible assets as they are something we can see and touch. Intangible assets are assets that are not physical in nature. The most common intangible asset is goodwill.

 brilliant definition

Goodwill occurs when one business buys another. It is the amount of money over and above the book value of the net assets of a firm that a buyer is willing to pay.

For example, assume you pay £7.5 million for a business that has net assets totalling £6 million. You pay over the odds by £1.5 million because the business has built up a good reputation and product range. Assuming the purchase price of £7.5 million is paid in cash, the ledger entries would be something like this:

> Debit: Plant, property and equipment £6 million
> Debit: Goodwill £1.5 million
> Credit: Bank £7.5 million

The balance sheet after the purchase of the new business thus will show goodwill as an intangible asset with a value of £1.5 million.

Current assets

Looking at the current assets of ABC plc, these are quite similar to those we have seen already. The only term not used before is *cash and cash equivalents*. This simply refers to cash held at the bank and other short-term deposits. It is a term recommended by accounting standards.

Equity

Earlier in this chapter, the owner's interest in a business was called capital. In a public or private company the owners are called shareholders. More specifically, holders of ordinary shares are the owners.

brilliant definition

An *ordinary share* (in the USA known as common stock) gives the holder partial ownership of a company. Holders of ordinary shares are entitled to voting rights in proportion to their holding.

As ordinary shareholders have voting rights they are entitled to attend the annual general meeting (AGM) of a company. An AGM is a gathering of the directors and shareholders of every company, required by law to be held each calendar year.

Only public companies can issue shares to the public. The ordinary shares sold are shown in the balance sheet as equity share capital – a total of £187 million on the balance sheet of ABC plc shown in Figure 9.11.

Ordinary shareholders may be paid a return called a dividend, but there is no right to any return. Preference shares, meanwhile, give a fixed return.

brilliant definition

A *preference share* is a share that pays a regular and fixed return. Preference shareholders have a claim on the profits of a company before ordinary shareholders. Normally, preference shares do not carry any voting rights.

The balance sheet of ABC plc in Figure 9.11 shows £1 million worth of preference shares, which is relatively a lot less than the equity share capital. This is quite typical, as companies don't want to commit to high fixed interest payments.

Shares are issued at their nominal (or par) value, which might be £1, for example. Investors might be willing to pay a lot more than this price as they will take account of both the past and future performance of the company. In accounting, shares are always shown in the balance sheet at nominal value. Any additional amount received is shown as a share premium. On the balance sheet of ABC plc, the share premium is £2,420 million, which is quite a bit more than the £188 million in equity and preference shares. It is not unusual to see a large share premium in the balance sheet of a successful public company as shareholders are willing to pay over the odds in the hope of obtaining a good return in the future.

Retained income is also shown under the equity heading. This is simply the profits that have been kept in the company over time. When a company makes a profit it can choose to pay some, all, or none of the profit to shareholders as a dividend. A dividend is a distribution of a company's profit to shareholders. Dividends may be paid out on a quarterly or six-monthly basis. They usually are not shown on the income statement, but as an attached note to the financial statements.

Liabilities

As with a sole trader, liabilities are also split between non-current and current. On the balance sheet of ABC plc in Figure 9.11, trade payables and bank loans are shown. They are divided between non-current and current depending on when they are due for payment – that is, within one year or after one year. Just one item needs a little more explanation.

Current income tax

The liability for income tax on the balance sheet of ABC plc is simply the amount of corporation tax owed to the taxation authorities. As taxation is calculated based on profits at the accounting year-end, a liability will exist in the balance sheet until it is paid.

 brilliant recap

- The income statement shows the profit or loss made in an accounting period.

- Profits and losses affect the capital of a business.

- The balance sheet shows the financial position of a business, i.e. the assets, liabilities and capital.

- The process of preparing an income statement and/or balance sheet begins from the trial balance.

- Adjustments such as closing inventory value, depreciation, accruals/prepayments and provisions are made often before an income statement/balance sheet is prepared.

- The financial statements of companies are similar in principle to those of sole traders, but the layout and content are dictated by accounting rules and company law.

PART 4

Checks on your book-keeping

CHAPTER 10

Keeping everything right

N ow that we've covered the main book-keeping tasks, this final chapter looks at what you need to do if and when the books of account in a business are subject to inspection by an external person(s). If you have followed this book, you should be well on the way to ensuring that the work you have done is of a reasonable standard.

In general, book-keeping work will be checked at least once per year by an accountant or auditor. If a business is a sole trader, then it is possible that an accountant prepares the financial statements at year-end only. This also may be the case for smaller companies, whereas larger companies most likely will have internal accountants and also engage external auditors to verify the financial statements. The role of an auditor has already been mentioned in Chapter 9. It is also possible that a business is subject to an audit by the tax authorities such as HM Revenue & Customs. An audit is possible for any of the taxes for which a business is registered (e.g. VAT, PAYE, etc.), or a full audit of all taxes.

Most businesses get really worried when they receive notification of a tax audit, but usually there is nothing to worry about. This is because, if you follow good book-keeping practices and the additional advice given in this chapter, the chance of getting an audit are extremely low – maybe once in the lifetime of a business owner/manager. If you don't, however, then alarm bells may be set off that trigger an audit and these tend to be much more focused and typically find something odd or incorrect.

For the rest of this chapter we'll focus on what you should do if an audit by the tax authorities happens in your business. Not all tasks in preparing for an audit are the responsibility of a book-keeper, but remember that all accounting comes back to the recording of daily transactions in the day books. Of course, the points made are equally relevant to preparing for the annual visit by external auditors. Some additional tasks you might need to do for the auditors are mentioned towards the end of the chapter.

What is a tax audit?

In earlier chapters, you saw how a business might be registered for taxes like VAT and PAYE. It may also be registered for income tax or corporation tax. While beyond the scope of this book, income tax refers to tax on income that is non-PAYE. For example, the profit made by a sole trader is subject to income tax in the same way that a job is to PAYE taxes. Corporation tax is paid on company profits.

In simple terms, a tax audit is a cross-check of the information and figures shown by you in your tax returns against those shown in your business records. As we have seen in Chapters 4 and 6, the day books are used as a source of information to complete VAT and PAYE returns. Thus, the basic aim of a tax audit is to ensure that 1. the day books and other records are accurate and 2. the amounts reported to the tax authorities are equal to these records.

Normally, a single tax inspector or official will conduct an audit at the business premises. More staff may be involved if the size of the business merits it. You will be informed in advance of the date of the audit, which you can change if it does not suit your schedule. You will also be informed of what taxes the audit will examine. In smaller businesses, the audit may also examine the personal tax affairs of the owner(s). Remember that the business entity concept (see Chapter 1) means that personal and business affairs are separate. For example, a partnership might be audited, with the tax affairs of each partner as an individual also subject to audit.

Typically, businesses are selected for a tax audit using one of the following three selection criteria.

1 *Screening tax returns*
   The vast majority of audits are selected in this way. Screening involves examining the returns made by a business and reviewing its compliance history – compliance means filing returns on time and paying taxes when due. Figures on returns are analysed in the light of trends and patterns in the particular business or sector.

2 *Projects on business sectors*

From time to time, projects are conducted to examine tax compliance levels in particular business sectors. The returns for a large number of businesses in a particular sector are screened in detail and a proportion of these are selected for audit. For example, many independent contractors have been the focus of audits from HM Revenue & Customs in the UK in recent years. The focus of these audits is to establish whether these individuals are in fact employees and should be in the PAYE system.

3 *Random selection*

This is in addition to the two methods mentioned above. It means that all businesses have a possibility of being audited. A very small proportion of audits are selected using this method.

Preparing for a tax audit

If you remember back to Chapter 3, you should invoice your customers without delay to avoid giving any extra credit. If you do this, your sales day book and associated ledgers should always be up to date. This applies for all other business transactions too, so you should always have an up-to-date set of records. This is the starting point for any tax audit. If your records are not fully up to date, you need to get things in order as soon as possible.

> you should always have an up-to-date set of records

brilliant tip

One sure way to keep up to date is to do a bank reconciliation statement (see Chapter 5) each month when you receive the bank statements. You'll need to have all records in order before you can do this, so it forces you to keep your books in an orderly fashion.

Assuming your records are in order, the next step is to get yourself prepared for the day of the audit. The best thing to do is take out the relevant records and have them ready in a separate file for the tax inspector. You will have been informed of the tax/taxes to be audited and the period of time. So, for example, if the audit covers PAYE records for 2008 and

2009, have these ready. Remember, too, that the records might include other day books or computer reports you might not think of in the first instance. For example, in a PAYE audit the cheque payments book and the petty cash book might be checked to see if payments were made to employees that were not recorded in the payroll records.

The next step you should do is a general review of the business. While an audit may focus on a specific tax, sometimes it can lead to a much broader examination of the books and/or the tax affairs of the owner.

brilliant example

If an audit of PAYE taxes is undertaken, then the full payroll records will be made available to the tax inspectors. For example, if the wages or drawings of the business owners were low, this might prompt an inspector to look further for 'undeclared' income. This would broaden the scope from PAYE to income tax and possibly also to VAT if the undeclared income was in fact cash sales which were unrecorded.

Some things to think about in doing a general review of the business include the following:

- Is the turnover (i.e. sales) of the business reflective of the underlying profits the business makes?
- Are all cash receipts recorded and banked? In other words, particularly in a cash business, ensure that the cash recorded as passing through the cash registers is accounted for by means of a cash book showing any payments out before cash is lodged.
- Do a quick sum of the sales and purchases you have reported on the VAT returns (see Chapter 4 and the VAT 100 form, page 64). Compare these totals with your sales and purchases day book totals (or the totals from your accounting software).
- In a sole trader or partnership, are drawings adequate for the lifestyle of the owner/partner?
- Are all expenditures vouched for? In other words, are all expenses related back to a proper source document, e.g. a purchase invoice or an expense report? Check the purchases day book and/or the

cheque payments book to ensure all expenses are supported by an appropriate source document.

- Have any personal expenses been classified as business expenses?
- Are all wages paid adequate and reflective of the work done by employees? If not, this could suggest that cash is being paid 'under the counter' to employees.

If you find anything wrong, don't try to cover it up. All book-keepers and accountants can make mistakes and you'll often find these when combing back over the books. If the monetary value of any error is small, a tax inspector or external auditor will not be too worried. If, however, there is a problem then the best thing to do is to be upfront and admit it. For example, let's assume you are a sole trader and haven't been recording all cash sales, instead keeping a sizeable portion for yourself. By doing this, the drawings figure is too low for the fact that you have a mortgage, partner, two kids and two cars. Let's say you know you have not recorded £20,000 in cash sales in a year, and by putting this in the business the drawings figure would look much better. If you declare this £20,000 to the tax inspector, yes you will have to pay income tax and possibly also VAT that you should have paid before. But, more importantly, you may avoid paying additional penalties and/or interest. HM Revenue & Customs and Ireland's Revenue Commissioners apply what is quite a fair approach to penalties. The approach taken depends on how 'bad' the taxpayer's (i.e. the business) behaviour has been. Here's what HM Revenue & Customs says:

if there is a problem be upfront and admit it

Penalties are charged as a percentage of the extra tax due. The rate increases according to how 'bad' a taxpayer's behaviour has been:

- *No penalties apply if 'reasonable care' has been taken*
- *Up to 30% for 'careless behaviour'*
- *Up to 70% for 'deliberate mistakes'*
- *Up to 100% for 'deliberate and concealed mistakes'*

You can read more about this at http://www.hmrc.gov.uk/about/new-penalties/penalties-leaflet.pdf. You can see how the approach leans much more heavily on businesses that deliberately conceal things. By the way, a 100% penalty means that any tax found to be due in the course of an audit is doubled.

Avoiding a tax audit

Of course, if you have read this book and apply the concepts herein, you should be quite confident that, if your business or workplace is the subject of a tax audit, your book-keeping will present few issues. Keeping a 'clean' up-to-date set of books is always the best thing to do. Don't worry about making mistakes, anyone can, and these should not present any major issues. Thinking back to earlier chapters, you have seen ways to verify your book-keeping with external sources, such as the bank reconciliation and checking your supplier accounts against statements that suppliers send you. In addition, there are some further steps you can take to avoid being selected for a tax audit, as follows:

● Pay taxes and file returns on time. Use online filing if possible as this speeds things up and you may also get more time to pay taxes due.

● If there are unusual figures in any return made to tax authorities, why not take a little time to explain them. For example, sales and profit might fall due to increased competition, not because sales are unrecorded.

● Seek professional advice if you need to. Book-keepers typically hand over their work to accountants for preparation of the financial statements at least once a year, but don't be afraid to call on an accountant at any time.

keeping things tidy and timely is best

Keeping things tidy and timely is the best way to minimise the chances of a tax audit. It does not eliminate the possibility but, if selected, your business should be fine.

Preparing for a visit by external auditors

An external auditor is a person(s), usually an accountant, who verifies financial statements of a limited company. External auditors do not always prepare financial statements; accountants do. Of course, an accountant can also be an external auditor and this is typically so in smaller accounting firms.

In the UK, not all companies are required by law to have an auditor. If turnover is less than £5.6 million and the balance sheet total is less than £2.8 million, then no audit is required. This does not mean such companies won't have auditors, as sometimes institutions like banks will insist on having 'audited' financial statements, meaning that an auditor verifies them as an accurate reflection of the books of account. All other companies require an auditor to certify the financial statements as being accurate.

So what does an auditor actually do? Let's assume you are employed as book-keeper in a company alongside an accountant. The accountant pre-pares monthly accounts for the managers of the business and, at year-end, produces the financial statements as required by law. Once the financial statements are done, the auditor then sets about doing checks and tests to ensure that 1. the financial statements are accurate and 2. they represent fairly the underlying books of account. No doubt, as book-keeper the auditor would examine some of your work. Here are some of the tests an auditor might do (it is by no means an exhaustive list).

● Conduct a 'walk-through' test. This means that the auditor takes a source document from beginning to end through the book-keeping and accounting system.

● Conduct a validity test. This means confirming that what is reflected in the accounting records or financial statements is real and actually exists.

● Undertake tests to ensure the completeness of the financial statements.

 brilliant definition

An *audit test* refers to activities conducted by an auditor to assess the accuracy of account balances and, in turn, financial statements.

As you might guess by the use of the word 'test', an auditor cannot examine any transactions. (S)he will take a sample of transactions and use these as the basis for tests. There are of course risks associated with choosing a sample, the most obvious being that any sample transactions are not reflective of the majority. Auditors will select a sample number of transactions which will minimise the risk. The following example gives some practical details of the audit test types above.

brilliant example

Here are some examples of audit tests.

1 Walk-through test. An auditor might want to test the sale processes. This would start with a sales order from a customer. The price charged on the invoice would be checked against that agreed on the sales order. The invoice would be traced to the sales day book and to the accounts receivable (sales) and nominal ledgers. Payment from the customer would also be traced through the cash receipts book, the ledgers and finally verified on the bank statement.

2 Validity test. The auditor might choose an asset from the asset register (see Chapter 7) and check its physical location and condition. This is to ensure that the asset actually exists.

3 Completeness test. The auditor will send a letter to the business's bank branch asking for details of the balances on the business bank accounts at the end of the financial year. This not only verifies the bank balance but also ensures that all bank accounts have in fact been revealed by the business.

As you can see from the audit tests described, the book-keeper is likely to be asked to provide documentation to help the auditor complete the tests. Many book-keepers fear the annual visit by auditors. They view it as someone 'checking up' on them. Why not look at the visit in a positive light, as it provides external validation of any work you've done. You can then be reasonably sure you are doing a good job.

brilliant recap

- A tax audit is when the tax authorities visit a business with the purpose of determining whether the records of the business agree with information submitted on various tax returns.

- Tax audits tend to be focused, with some form of screening used to select the business for audit.

- The best preparation for a tax audit is a clean, well-organised set of accounting records.

- If you have something to tell the tax authorities, be upfront, as it can save you a lot of money in penalties.

- The best way to avoid a tax audit is to comply with dates for filing tax returns and paying taxes.

- External auditors may interact with book-keepers while conducting tests as part of the annual audit of a company.

Glossary

Account: A section in a ledger devoted to a single aspect of a business (e.g. a bank account, wages account, office expenses account).

Accounting cycle: Covers everything from opening the books at the start of the year to closing them at the end. In other words, everything you need to do in one accounting year accounting-wise.

Accounting equation: The formula used to prepare a balance sheet: assets = liabilities + equity.

Accounts payable: An account in the nominal ledger that contains the overall balance of the purchase ledger.

Accounts payable ledger: A subsidiary ledger that holds the accounts of a business's suppliers. A single control account is held in the nominal ledger, which shows the total balance of all the accounts in the purchase ledger.

Accounts receivable: An account in the nominal ledger that contains the overall balance of the sales ledger.

Accounts receivable ledger: A subsidiary ledger that holds the accounts of a business's customers. A single control account is held in the nominal ledger, which shows the total balance of all the accounts in the sales ledger.

Accruals: If, during the course of a business, certain charges are incurred but no invoice is received then these charges are referred to as accruals (they 'accrue' or increase in value). A typical example is interest payable on a loan where you have not yet received a bank statement. These items (or an estimate of their value) should still be included in the profit and loss account. When the real invoice is received, an adjustment can be made to correct the estimate. Accruals also can apply to the income side.

Accrual method of accounting: Most businesses use the accrual method of accounting (because usually it is required by accounting regulations and the law). When you issue an invoice on credit (ie. regardless of whether it is paid or not), it is treated as a taxable supply on the date it was issued for income tax purposes (or corporation tax for limited companies). The same applies to bills received from suppliers. (This does not mean you pay income tax immediately, just that it must be included in that year's profit and loss account.)

Accumulated depreciation account: An account held in the nominal ledger that holds the depreciation of a fixed asset until the end of the asset's useful life (because it has been either scrapped or sold). It is credited each year with that year's depreciation, hence the balance increases (i.e. accumulates) over a period of time. Each fixed asset will have its own accumulated depreciation account.

Arrears: Bills that should have been paid. For example, if you have forgotten to pay your last three months' rent, then you are said to be three months in arrears on your rent.

Assets: Represent what a business owns or what is due. Equipment, vehicles, buildings, creditors, money in the bank, cash are all examples of the assets of a business. Typical breakdown includes 'fixed assets', 'current assets' and 'non-current assets'. Fixed refers to equipment, buildings, plant, vehicles, etc. Current refers to cash, money in the bank, debtors, etc. Non-current assets are the same as fixed assets.

At cost: The 'at cost' price usually refers to the price originally paid for something, as opposed to, say, the retail price.

Audit: The process of checking every entry in a set of books to make sure they agree with the original paperwork (e.g. checking a journal's entries against the original purchase and sales invoices).

Audit trail: A list of transactions in the order they occurred. Most accounting software can readily provide an automatic audit trail report.

Bad debts account: An account in the nominal ledger to record the value of unrecoverable debts from customers. Real bad debts or those that are likely to happen can be deducted as expenses against tax liability (provided they refer specifically to a customer).

Balance sheet: A summary of all the accounts of a business. Usually prepared at the end of each financial year. The term 'balance sheet' implies that the combined balances of assets exactly equals the liabilities and equity.

Bill: A term typically used to describe a purchase invoice (e.g. an invoice from a supplier).

Bought ledger: See purchase ledger.

Capital: An amount of money put into the business (often by way of a loan) as opposed to money earned by the business.

Capital assets: See fixed assets.

Cash accounting: This term describes an accounting method whereby only invoices and bills that have been paid are accounted for. However, for most types of business in the UK, as far as the Inland Revenue is concerned, as soon as you issue an invoice (paid or not) it is treated as revenue and must be accounted for. An exception is VAT: Customs & Excise normally require you to account for VAT on an accrual basis. However, there is an option called 'cash accounting' whereby only paid items are included as far as VAT is concerned (e.g. if most of your sales are on credit, you may benefit from this scheme – contact your local Customs & Excise office for the current rules and turnover limits).

Cash book: A journal in which cash sales and purchases are entered. A cash book can also be used to record the transactions of a bank account.

Cash in hand: See undeposited funds account.

Chart of accounts: A list of all the accounts held in the nominal ledger.

Closing the books: A term used to describe the journal entries necessary to close the sales and expense accounts of a business at year-end by posting their balances to the profit and loss account, and ultimately to close the profit and loss account too by posting its balance to a capital or other account.

Compensating error: A double-entry term applied to a mistake that has cancelled out another mistake.

Control account: An account held in a ledger that summarises the balance of all the accounts in the same or another ledger. Typically each subsidiary ledger will have a control account, which will be mirrored by another control account in the nominal ledger.

Cook the books: Falsify a set of accounts. See also creative accounting.

Cost accounting: An area of management accounting that deals with the costs of a business in terms of enabling the management to manage the business more effectively.

Cost of sales: A formula for working out the direct costs of your sales (including stock) over a particular period. The result represents the gross profit. The formula is: opening stock + purchases + direct expenses − closing stock. Also called cost of goods sold when goods are manufactured for re-sale, rather than bought.

Creative accounting: A questionable means of making company figures appear more (or less) appealing to shareholders, bankers, etc.

Credit: A column in a journal or ledger to record the 'from' side of a transaction (e.g. if you buy some petrol using a cheque then the money is paid from the bank to the petrol account and you would therefore credit the bank when making the journal entry).

Credit note: A sales invoice in reverse. A typical example is where you issue an invoice for £100: the customer then returns £25 worth of the goods, so you issue the customer with a credit note to say that you owe the customer £25.

Creditors: A list of suppliers to whom the business owes money.

Creditors control account: An account in the nominal ledger that contains the overall balance of the purchase ledger.

Current assets: Include money in the bank, petty cash, money received but not yet banked (see cash in hand), money owed to the business by its customers, raw materials for manufacturing, and stock bought for re-sale. They are termed 'current' because they are active accounts. Money flows in and out of them each financial year and we will need frequent reports of their balances if the business is to survive (e.g. 'do we need more stock and have we got enough money in the bank to buy it?').

Current liabilities: Include bank overdrafts, short-term loans (less than a year) and what the business owes its suppliers. They are termed 'current' for the same reasons outlined under 'current assets'.

Customs & Excise: The government department usually responsible for collecting sales tax (e.g. VAT in the UK).

Day books: A book or set of books where your transactions are entered first. Examples are the purchases day book, sales day book, cash receipts book and cheque payments book.

Debit: A column in a journal or ledger to record the 'to' side of a transaction (e.g. if you are paying money into your bank account you would debit the bank when making the journal entry).

Debtors: A list of customers who owe money to the business.

Debtors control account: An account in the nominal ledger that contains the overall balance of the sales ledger.

Depreciation: The value of assets usually decreases as time goes by. The amount or percentage it decreases by is called depreciation. This normally is calculated at the end of every accounting period (usually a year) at a typical percentage rate of its last value. It is shown in both the profit and loss account and balance sheet of a business. See straight-line depreciation.

Double-entry book-keeping: A system that accounts for every aspect of a transaction – where it came from and where it went to. This *from* and *to* aspect of a transaction (called crediting and debiting) is what the term double-entry means. Modern double-entry dates back to the fifteenth century.

Drawings: Money taken out of a business by its owner(s) for personal use. This is entirely different to wages paid to a business's employees or the wages or remuneration of a limited company's directors (see wages).

Entry: Part of a transaction recorded in a journal or posted to a ledger.

Equity: The value of the business to the owner(s) of the business (which is the difference between the business's assets and liabilities).

Error of commission: A double-entry term that means one or both sides of a double entry have been posted to the wrong account (but are within the same class of account). For example: petrol expense posted to vehicle maintenance expense.

Error of omission: A double-entry term that means a transaction has been omitted entirely from the books.

Error of original entry: A double-entry term that means a transaction has been entered with the wrong amount.

Error of principle: A double-entry term that means one or both sides of a double entry have been posted to the wrong account (which is also a different class of account). For example: petrol expense posted to fixtures and fittings.

Expenses: Goods or services purchased directly for the running of the business. This does not include goods bought for re-sale or any items of a capital nature.

Fiscal year: Term used for a business's accounting year. The period is usually 12 months, which can begin during any month of the calendar year (e.g. 1 April 2008 to 31 March 2009).

Fixed assets: See non-current assets.

Fixtures and fittings: Class of fixed asset that includes office furniture, filing cabinets, display cases, warehouse shelving and the like.

General ledger: See nominal ledger.

Goodwill: An extra value placed on a business if the owner of a business decides it is worth more than the value of its assets. It is included usually where the business is to be sold as a going concern.

Gross loss: The difference between sales and cost of sales, assuming cost of sales is greater than sales.

Gross margin: The difference between the selling price of a product or service and the cost of that product or service, often shown as a percentage.

E.g. if a product sold for £100 and cost £60 to buy or manufacture, the gross margin would be 40 per cent.

Gross profit: The difference between sales and cost of sales, assuming sales is greater than cost of sales.

Impersonal accounts: Accounts not held in the name of persons (i.e. they do not relate directly to a business's customers and suppliers).

Imprest system: A method of topping up petty cash. A fixed sum of petty cash is placed in the petty cash box. When the petty cash balance is nearing zero, it is topped up to its original level again.

Income: Money received by a business from its commercial activities. See revenue.

Income statement: A financial statement made up of revenue and expense accounts that shows the current profit or loss of a business (i.e. whether a business has earned more than it has spent in the current year). Often referred to as a profit and loss account or P&L.

Inland Revenue: The government department usually responsible for collecting your tax.

Insolvent: A company is insolvent if it has insufficient funds (all of its assets) to pay its debts (all of its liabilities). If a company's liabilities are greater than its assets and it continues to trade, it is not only insolvent but, in the UK, is operating illegally.

Intangible assets: Assets of a non-physical or financial nature. An asset such as goodwill is a good example. See tangible assets.

Invoice: A term describing an original document either issued by a business for the sale of goods on credit (a sales invoice) or received by the business for goods bought (a purchase invoice).

Journal(s): See day books.

Journal entries: A term used to describe the transactions recorded in a journal.

Ledger: A book in which entries posted from the journals are reorganised into accounts.

Liabilities: Include bank overdrafts, loans taken out for the business and money owed by the business to its suppliers. Liabilities are included in the balance sheet and normally consist of accounts that have a credit balance.

Long-term liabilities: Usually refer to long-term loans (i.e. a loan that lasts for more than one year such as a mortgage).

Loss: See net loss.

Management accounting: Accounts and reports are tailor-made for the use of the managers and directors of a business (in any form they see fit – there are no rules) as opposed to financial accounts, which are prepared for the Inland Revenue and any other parties not directly connected with the business. See also cost accounting.

Memorandum accounts: A name for the accounts held in a subsidiary ledger, e.g. the accounts in a sales ledger.

Narrative: A comment appended to an entry in a journal. It can be used to describe the nature of the transaction and often, in particular, where the other side of the entry went to (or came from).

Net loss: The value of expenses less sales, assuming that the expenses are greater.

Net price: The price less any tax, e.g. VAT.

Net profit: The value of sales less expenses, assuming that the sales are greater.

Net worth: See equity.

Nominal accounts: A set of accounts held in the nominal ledger. They are termed 'nominal' because they don't usually relate to an individual person.

Nominal ledger: A ledger that holds all the nominal accounts of a business. Where the business uses a subsidiary ledger like the sales ledger to hold customer details, the nominal ledger usually will include a control account to show the total balance of the subsidiary ledger (a control account can be termed 'nominal' because it doesn't relate to a specific person).

Non-current assets: Anything that a business owns or buys for use within the business and that retains a value over a number of years. They usually consist of major items like land, buildings, equipment and vehicles but can include smaller items like tools (see depreciation).

Opening the books: Every time a business closes the books for a year, it opens a new set. The new set of books will be empty, therefore the balances from the last balance sheet must be copied into them (via journal entries) so that the business is ready to start the new year.

Ordinary share: A type of share issued by a limited company. It carries the highest risk but usually attracts the highest rewards.

Original book of entry: A book that contains the details of the day-to-day transactions of a business (see journal).

Overheads: The costs involved in running a business. They consist entirely of expense accounts (e.g. rent, insurance, petrol, staff wages, etc.).

PAYE: 'Pay as you earn'. The name given to the income tax system where an employee's tax and National Insurance contributions are deducted before the wages are paid.

Personal accounts: The accounts of a business's customers and suppliers. They usually are held in the sales and purchase ledgers.

Petty cash: A small amount of money held in reserve (normally used to purchase items of small value where a cheque or other form of payment is not suitable).

Posting: The copying of entries from the journals to the ledgers.

Preference share: A type of share issued by a limited company. It carries a medium risk but has the advantage over ordinary shares in that preference shareholders get the first slice of the dividend 'pie', but usually at a fixed rate.

Prepayments: One or more accounts set up to account for money paid in advance (e.g. insurance, where part of the premium applies to the current financial year and the remainder to the following year).

Profit and loss account: See income statement.

Profit margin: The percentage difference between the cost of a product and the price you sell it for. For example, if a product costs you £10 to buy and you sell it for £20, then you have a 100 per cent profit margin. This is known also as your 'mark-up'.

Pro-forma invoice: An invoice sent that requires payment before any goods or services have been despatched.

Provisions: One or more accounts set up to account for expected future payments, e.g. where a business is expecting a bill but hasn't received it yet.

Purchase ledger: A subsidiary ledger that holds the accounts of a business's suppliers. A single control account is held in the nominal ledger, which shows the total balance of all the accounts in the purchase ledger.

Raw materials: The materials bought by a manufacturing business in order to manufacture its products.

Receipt: A term typically used to describe confirmation of a payment – if you buy some petrol, normally you will ask for a receipt to prove that the money was spent legitimately.

Reconciling: The procedure of checking entries made in a business's books with those on a statement sent by a third person, e.g. checking a bank statement against your own records.

Refund: If you return some goods you have just bought (for whatever reason), the company you bought them from may give you your money back.

Retail: A term usually applied to a shop that re-sells goods. This type of business will require a trading account as well as a profit and loss account.

Retained earnings: The amount of money held in a business after its owner(s) have taken their share of the profits.

Revenue: The sales and any other taxable income of a business, e.g. interest earned from money on deposit.

Sales: Income received from selling goods or a service. See revenue.

Sales invoice: See invoice.

Sales ledger: A subsidiary ledger that holds the accounts of a business's customers. A control account is held in the nominal ledger (usually called a debtors control account), which shows the total balance of all the accounts in the sales ledger.

Service: A term usually applied to a business that sells a service rather than manufactures or sells goods, e.g. an architect or a window cleaner.

Shareholders: The owners of a limited company.

Shares: Documents issued by a company to its owners (the shareholders) that state how many shares in the company each shareholder has bought and what percentage of the company the shareholder owns. Shares can also be called 'stock'.

SME: Small and medium enterprises (i.e. small and medium size businesses). The distinction between what is small and what is medium varies depending on where you are and who you talk to.

Sole proprietor: The self-employed owner of a business.

Sole trader: See sole proprietor.

Source document: An original invoice, bill or receipt to which journal entries refer.

Stock taking: Physically checking a business's stock for total quantities and value.

Stock valuation: Valuing a stock of goods bought for manufacturing or re-sale.

Straight-line depreciation: Depreciating something by the same (i.e. fixed) amount every year rather than as a percentage of its previous value. For example, a vehicle initially costs £10,000. If you depreciate it at a rate of £2,000 a year, it will depreciate to zero in exactly 5 years. See depreciation.

Subsidiary ledgers: Ledgers opened in addition to a business's nominal ledger. They are used to keep sections of a business separate from each other.

T account: A particular method of displaying an account where the debits and associated information are shown on the left, and credits and associated information on the right.

Tangible assets: Assets of a physical nature. Examples include buildings, motor vehicles, plant and equipment, fixtures and fittings.

Trading account: An account that shows the gross profit or loss of a manufacturing or retail business, i.e. sales less the cost of sales. It can be prepared before the profit and loss account, but is included more often as the first portion of the profit and loss account/income statement.

Transaction: Two or more entries made in a journal which, when looked at together, reflect an original document such as a sales invoice or purchase receipt.

Trial balance: A statement showing all the accounts used in a business and their balances.

Turnover: The income of a business over a period of time (usually a year).

Undeposited funds account: An account used to show the current total of money received not yet banked. This can include money, cheques, credit card payments, banker's drafts, etc. This type of account is also commonly referred to as a 'cash in hand' account.

Value added tax (VAT): A sales tax that increases the price of goods. At the time of writing the UK VAT standard rate is 17.5%. There is also a rate for fuel, which is 5% (this refers to heating fuels like coal, electricity and gas and not road fuels like petrol, which is still rated at 17.5%). VAT is added to the price of goods, so in the UK, an item that sells at £10 will be priced £11.75 when 17.5% VAT is added.

Wages: Payments made to the employees of a business for their work on behalf of the business. These are classed as expense items and must not be confused with 'drawings' taken by sole proprietors and partnerships.

Work in progress: The value of partly finished/manufactured goods.

Write-off: Depreciating an asset to zero in one go.